THE TRUE CONFESSIONS OF
WILLIAM OWEN
SMUGGLER, PRIVATEER AND MURDERER

Title page of manuscript of Owen's confessions

The True Confessions of
William Owen
Smuggler, Privateer and Murderer

Terry Breverton

Gwasg Carreg Gwalch

First publication: 2018

ISBN: 978-1-84524-283-1

Cover design: Eleri Owen
Cover image: A Revenue Cruiser chasing a Smuggling Lugger –
Charles Dixon (1872-1934)

Published by Gwasg Carreg Gwalch,
12 Iard yr Orsaf, Llanrwst, Wales LL26 0EH
tel: 01492 642031
email: books@carreg-gwalch.cymru
website: www.carreg-gwalch.cymru

Printed and published in Wales

Cyflwynedig i
Glyn Parry

This book could never have been written without the invaluable researches of two men. The tireless Glyn Parry, former archivist at the National Library of Wales, Aberystwyth, whose work initiated this project, gave me a huge file of previous work on Owen, assisted me many times in that library, and pointed me to, and helped transcribe, important documents. Equally, I must thank Dr. Paul Muskett, whose research in the Manx National Heritage Library and in the *Atholl Archive* at Blair Castle has been made freely available. Diolch yn fawr!

Contents

Preface

This author finds it easy to write non-fiction, assisted by three factors. A background in consultancy and acadaemia assists research capabilities. Also having my own computer since 1984 (– a Ferranti 86B, when UK firms still designed and made things), I was able to retrieve and store information, a process made easier every year. The third factor is a genuine desire for knowledge – an attribute multiplied by this writer's form of attention deficit disorder, which make me uncomfortable not knowing something. I always want to discover new things, for instance in my biography of Black Bart Roberts I found out that the 'deceased' Israel Hands, a member of Blackbeard's crew, later sailed under Roberts, and was hung in chains with the other seventeen most important of Black Bart's pirates. Equally, it is interesting that only five factual pirates were mentioned in *Treasure Island* – Captain Edward England (who sailed and argued with Roberts in the Indian Ocean); the aforesaid Israel Hands; the two Welsh captains, Roberts and Howell Davis; and Roberts' Welsh surgeon, Peter Scudamore, who was said by R.L. Stevenson to have amputated Long John Silver's leg. So writing is 'easy' – it allows one to go off at tangents, become lost in another world and absorbs time that might otherwise be wasted in a tavern.

This is what I thought – research and writing were simple – until I was asked to write a straightforward 25,000 word book upon William Owen, a noted smuggler hung in 1747. What could be easier? An 1811 copy of his death cell confessions existed at the National Library of Wales, Aberystwyth, along with a preçis of his life identifying him as the son of Owen David Bowen of Nevern. I checked the Nevern parish register, and found the person existed, and went on to try and discover who his parents were, and where they lived to be able to buy him two trading boats. After virtually completing the book, within the word limit, I had the good fortune to contact Dr Reginald Davies, who told me that this particular 'Guliemus filius Audoeni David Bowen' had died when a few months old. Many hours of further checking of existing Nevern and neighbouring parish records found no other William Owen of the period, although apart from Nevern few records remain. His confessions are substantially true, if overblown, except we cannot verify his career privateering in the West Indies, and instead he may have been impressed to serve there in the Royal Navy. Paul Muskett's researches in the Isle of Man and the North of England substantiate Owen's seemingly grandiose claims of fighting larger Customs cruisers, and his murder of the Customs officer at Cardigan is well documented. His sentence of manslaughter for that offence and quick release seems astonishing today. A couple of newspaper reports after his execution claimed Owen was a bigamist, and that seems true.

The other complicating factor, trying to disentangle truth from fiction, was his alliance with James Lilly, a man he had previously sued for £40. Most writings indicate that James, a fencing master, had a brother John, a dancing master and teacher of drawing, in Haverfordwest. However, John and James were eventually discovered to be the same man, and perhaps James sometimes used John to confuse his creditors and the law. Lilly married for money and seemed to have wasted it all. Having been sentenced to seven years transportation to the Americas, he escaped from Haverfordwest Gaol and met up with Owen, and the two took to burglary. With the hue and cry catching up with them, Lilly shot the leading chaser's horse, and Owen shot its rider. With only one horse between the pair, Owen then shot and killed Lilly and tried to escape over Llanllwni Mountain. By an odd coincidence, the field, Cae Lilly, where Lilly was shot, is near this author's favourite pub, the Eagle in Lanfihangel-ar-Arth. In the court transcript, this was Llanhenell, and no such place exists in West Wales, but Glyn Parry had discovered that the inhabitants of Llanfihangel-ar-Arth (then known as Llanfihangel Iorath) used to shorten it to a sound like Llaninel or Llanengel. The present offering is 50,000 words and could easily be twice the length – there are more skeins to untangle in the tortuous intertwining tale of this pair of rogues.

I have tried to simplify the story by giving a first chapter upon smuggling at the time, and the influence of the semi-independent Isle of Man, followed by a modernised transcript of Owen's 19,000 word confession and trial proceedings. There then follows a third chapter, the Reverend Vincent's 1860 tale of Owen, important for possibly giving us his true birthplace, but more so for leading me to James Lilly marrying Anne Laugharne of Llanreithan, which leads to a long footnote on Lilly. The fourth chapter is my attempt at a 'true' life of William Owen, to compare with his confession. It is followed by footnotes upon the scene of Lilly's murder, since known as Cae Lilly; upon the Rev John Davies who attended the condemned Owen; and on the Mathias family who had possession of, and copied, the original Owen manuscript. The book is completed by short chapters upon Carmarthen and Cardigan executions of the time; a near contemporary smuggling legend, Siôn Cwilt; and the Rebecca Rioter of Cae Lilly.

This has been a difficult detective story, following up many loose ends, and I hope it is easier to read than it has been to write. I leave it to others with far more genealogical experience than myself, to take up the baton of what happened to the families of Owen and Lilly. I was advised that I needed to research archives in Barbados for Owen's exploits in that place, so am open to offers of funding to travel there and spend a few weeks to that purpose.

Introduction

Sometimes one begins writing a book and it is almost complete, when everything falls apart and far, far more research is necessary. The author was convinced by other writings that William Owen was born in Nevern (Nanhyfer), but very late in the writing process discovered that particular person only lived a few months. The parish transcripts of Nevern are remarkably intact compared to surrounding parishes, and an exhaustive search could not find anything about Owen or his family in Nevern. However, the Owens were a powerful family in the area, and all their residences were studied, with Llangamon (Llangaman) being a likely birthplace, until Glyn Parry pointed me to an unpublished manuscript from c.1860. In it, the Reverend Henry Vincent of Newport Castle stated that Owen was born at Tŷ Hir, St Dogmael's, a neighbouring parish to Nevern. Known as Will Tyhir, a 'notorious freebooter', Vincent initially recorded him as Bowen. St Dogmael's records are virtually non-existent, and his home seems to have been demolished before Vincent's time. Vincent's recollections, gathered from locals, give a far less glamorous version of Owen's life than his *Confessions*. It also appears that a book on Owen was printed soon after his death, which may have been his actual *Confessions*, but no trace of it seems to have survived.

In July 1982 the National Library of Wales purchased a vellum manuscript (*NLW MS. 21834B*), the death cell confession and autobiography of a smuggler. Welsh criminal biographies of the period are rare, with Eiluned Rees, editor of *Libri Walliae* (– the bibliography of pre-1820 Welsh printed works), informing Glyn Parry that there are only about half a dozen prior biographies of convicted Welsh criminals. William Owen was captured on 6 April 1747 and wrote his confession after being sentenced to death upon 16 April, and before being hanged for murder at Carmarthen on 2 May. The confession and autobiography was either written by Owen himself (he was literate), or dictated to the Reverend John Davies (see Chapter 4, footnote 2), who attended on Owen during his last days in Carmarthen Gaol. Daniel James, William Owen's gaoler, rather than the Reverend John Davies, seems to have been the intended beneficiary of the manuscript. After its completion, it was handed to Daniel James, possibly in recompense for his expenses in maintaining Owen in prison. The autobiography states that James was 'a very hospitable man, took compassion upon him [Owen] and found him with necessaries' (*NLW MS 21834B, f.120*).

The original is lost, and the manuscript purchased by the National Library of Wales is a copy by Daniel G. Matthias (see Chapter 5, footnote 3), who signed inside the front cover, dating it to January 1811. Owen's confession is unusually frank, telling us of several illegitimate children, extra-marital affairs, visits to brothels, victories, privateering, smuggling exploits, defeats and killings. However, it is written in the third person, aggrandising himself as a much admired and intelligent man. Certain aspects were omitted by Owen, which are included in Chapter 4, a factual retelling of Owen's life from recent research. More is to be discovered, which I shall leave to more capable researchers.

Chapter 1

Smuggling in the Eighteenth Century

Large-scale smuggling started in the reign of Edward I (1272-1307), when a customs duty was placed upon the export of British wool, which was in great demand across Europe. Initial duties were small, but during the Hundred Years War the tax increased to fund armies. The Customs Service existed only to collect customs duties at ports, and not to prevent smuggling, but in the 17th and 18th centuries smuggling grew rapidly from small-scale evasion of duties, into an industry in its own right. In 1614 the export of wool was made illegal, and this led to smuggling of wool, known as 'owling' (after the owl-like noises made by the smugglers at night to communicate with each other and to ships). In 1661 this illegal export of wool was made punishable by death, and smugglers began arming themselves. Any armed prevention was carried out by the British Army, and in 1671 Charles II created the Board of Customs, responsible for the collection of customs duties. From the 1680s, Revenue Officers were provided with customs cutters, to patrol the coast to catch smugglers.

The term 'excise', meaning a tax upon certain goods or commodities, had been introduced in the mid-17th century under Cromwell. During the Civil War an excise tax covered many different goods, but was reduced ten years later to cover just luxury items such as chocolate, coffee, tea, beer and spirits. However it was an effective way of raising tax revenues, so governments re-introduced excise duty on essentials such as salt, leather and soap. Upon the Restoration of the Monarchy, many Puritan social restrictions had been overturned, but excise was re-introduced, under the Tenures Abolition Act of 1660, in lieu of rent for tenancies of royally owned land.

In the 18th century massive quantities of goods were smuggled into Britain, with whole communities in some areas becoming dependent upon smuggling. *Smuggling.co.uk* tells us 'A smuggler on a shopping trip was as keen as a modern day-tripper to save money, but 18th century bargains make our duty-free allowances look stingy. The profit margin varied with the prevailing rates of duty, but typically tea cost seven pence a pound (3p) on the continent, and could be sold in England for 5s (25p). Tobacco cost the same, and fetched 2/6 (12½ p) at home. A tub of gin or brandy cost £1, and found English customers at four pounds even before "letting down" to a drinkable strength. Diluted, the profit would have been even greater.'

The North Anglesey diarist William Bulkeley frequently bought smuggled goods. He bought French brandy at five shillings a gallon, and also white wine and good claret, from a Flintshire man operating between Wales and the Isle of Man. In 1750 Bulkeley wrote 'On account of a very penal law being passed last Session of Parliament against the running of soap and candles, there will soon be no soap to be had, but what comes from Chester at 7d a pound. I bought today off a woman in that business 20lb almost (which I am afraid is the last I shall have of

A Revenue Cruiser chasing a Smuggling Lugger – Charles Dixon (1872-1934)

her).' Goods smuggled into Anglesey moved to the mainland, and so much brandy passed through the island that the most popular drink there was *todi*, a sweetened concoction of brandy and water. Bulkeley's contemporary diarist, Parson Woodforde Bulkeley, JP at Beaumaris, also bought smuggled goods, and was lenient towards smugglers, always trying to discharge them without punishment. In Wales, there were few honest Excise men, and very little inclination among local gentry to prosecute them. Samuel Johnson gave a popular definition in his 1755 dictionary: 'EXCI'SE. n.s. ... A hateful tax levied upon commodities, and adjudged not by the common judges of property, but wretches hired by those to whom excise is paid.'

In 1745, William Owen's era, Owen Owens was the Excise man operating between the rivers Glaslyn and Dwyryd in Meirionnydd. He hardly ever reported any crime, but after 18 years, in 1763, the authorities pressurised him into action. Elias and Meirion report that in 1763 Owens 'seized the *Speedwell*, an 18-ton open boat from Deeside, which was smuggling gin and brandy from the Isle of Man. But the captain complained that Owens had been in cahoots with the smugglers all that time! As a result, Owens lost his job and was jailed for two years.' Smuggling was endemic along all the Welsh coastline in the 18th century, in common with most of the western coasts of England and Scotland.

Unfortunately, many records of customs houses were destroyed in an 1815 fire at the Thames-side Customs House. Customs and Excise duties and taxes were high, and the majority of the population, including the gentry and landowners, obviously preferred to pay as little as possible for certain goods. There was, indeed, a 'golden age' of smuggling throughout the eighteenth century, lasting until around 1850. Taxes were difficult to collect, and England's constant warring led to insufficient resources being deployed against the 'trade'.

Customs houses were set up at larger ports, but boats instead brought in their goods at smaller ports, remote coves, or roadsteads where they were ferried ashore, usually at night. Captains of merchant ships had to report to customs before unloading cargoes, but often had sold off the bulk of the shipment elsewhere before declaring. Possibly a third of all taxable goods escaped the taxation system, with spirits, wines, tea, tobacco, spices, lace, silk, salt and other highly taxed items being the most profitable. In 1729, it is thought that the government lost at least a quarter of the income that it could have earned from imports.

Taxes paid on land and property were difficult to evade, but excise duties on commodities indirectly burdened the consumer buying salt, soap, or beer. 'As Britain became engaged in expensive conflicts, so the number of taxes (especially indirect taxes) multiplied and the middle classes, as well as the poorer members of society, suffered... In these circumstances it became more difficult to impose new taxes in times of peace, despite an army of revenue officers' (– *National Archives*). Thus, income tax, first instituted in 1799 was used as a way to even

Smugglers on a beach – George Morland (1763–1804)
Goods were taken ashore in small boats and carted inland at night

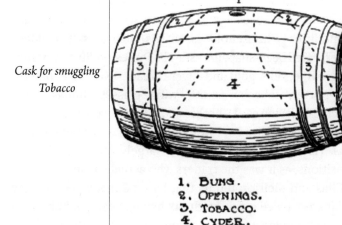

Cask for smuggling Tobacco

1. BUNG.
2. OPENINGS.
3. TOBACCO.
4. CYDER.

A copy of a 1782 smuggling reward poster

A SHIP HAS BEEN SIGHTED
in this quarter
ENGAGING IN THE UNLAWFUL ACT OF

SMUGGLING

whosoever can lay information
leading to the capture of this ship
or its crew
will receive a reward of

£500

From His Majesty's Government

This 19th day of October 1782

out the tax burden. In the eighteenth century, the commonest taxes paid were excise duties. They were levied on basic commodities – household essentials such as salt, candles, leather, corn, beer, soap, and starch. Duties on 'luxury' items, such as wine, silks, gold and silver thread, silver plate, brandy, rum, porter, tobacco, snuff, wine glasses, linens, hats, medicines, playing cards, horses and coaches were aimed at the rich. Parliament raised or lowered duties, as well as adding new items. However, consumers were largely unaware of these impositions, as it was the traders who actually paid.

Elias and Meirion tell us that by 1768 many people were drinking tea twice a day, 'with tax having been paid on just a little over a quarter of this amount.' In 1743, at the height of William Owen's 'career', tax was raised upon 650,000 pounds of tea, but it was estimated that 1,500,000 pounds was the annual consumption. At this time, except in rural communities, relying upon local clean wells, water was a dangerous commodity. Children drank 'small beer' and adults ale, as boiling removed many bacteria that cause diseases. Elias and Meirion state that in 1760 a pound of tea cost two shillings in Holland and ten shillings in Britain. They tell us that 96% of the price of tea was tax. 'A four gallon tub of French brandy cost fifteen shillings to buy on the continent, but on being imported to Britain would rise to a staggering £50!' In 1709 a candle tax came in, and the making of candles in the home was also forbidden unless one held a licence. Rush lighting was exempt. Rushes were dipped in animal fat then left to harden, and smelt badly. They could be lit at both ends, but only provided light for a very brief period of time – this is the origin of the saying 'to burn the candle at both ends'.

In 18th century London, the increase in the rate of consumption of gin led to an increased tax, and caused great riots in 1743. The tax upon wallpaper was overcome by the use of plain paper and stencils. The price of salt was four times what it cost in Ireland, plus there was 16% duty to be added, and it was desperately needed not just for cooking, but for preserving meat and butter, salting herrings etc. Ireland was a major source of rock-salt, and salt smuggling drew support from every part of the community. 'The tax on salt was a particular burden to the local fishing industry, which relied on salt for preservation. It was sold about 1s [5p] a pound about the first half of the [18th] century. There was also much smuggling carried on in the salt line, and the smugglers supplied the country with salt at 4d [1.5p] per lb. Their usual time for doing business was at night, and much liquor was supplied by the same traders at a low price.' (– Richard Platt). In William Owen's time, salt cost 4 pence a pound in England and Wales, but only a penny in Ireland. Smugglers sold it in Wales for 2 pence, making 100% mark-up, and in turn the buyers bought it at half-price. Members of the Salt Board travelled from port to port checking for salt smuggling, but it was generally carried on well away from such centres.

Customs houses were built in ports for the customs collector and other revenue officials, and to store confiscated goods. Revenue, or excise, men were appointed to catch smugglers, generally working from dusk until dawn. 'Searchers' were office-based officials who supervised officers, and often had substantial salaries for instructing officials in searching for hidden smuggled goods. Rewards of 50 % of the value of any recovered goods were shared, with the Searcher receiving a larger proportion. There were also 'Riding Officers' from 1698, supposedly stationed around every ten miles along the coast. If they sighted any suspicious activity, they were supposed to gather and apprehend any suspects, but most did little except fabricate their journals of activities. Many worked hand-in-hand with the smugglers in exchange for goods and no danger.

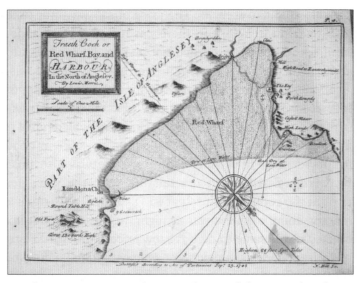

Anglesey was an important destination for smuggled continental goods via Ireland and Man

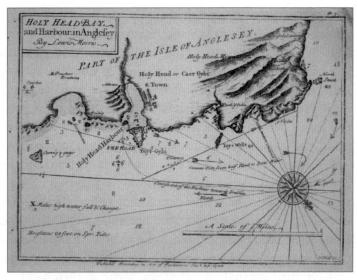

Smuggling via Anglesey reached its zenith in Owen's time with Welsh smugglers hiring Irish Wherries

They were very unpopular, being treated with contempt, because they angered people by their searches of their homes, farm outbuildings, and even surrounding fields in search of contraband.

Revenue officers in ports were known as 'landwaiters', who inspected foreign goods when they were unloaded, and made sure that all duties were paid. 'Coastwaiters' or 'Coastal Waiters' inspected goods transported from other British ports. 'Coal Masters' were in charge of collecting the tax on coal as it was moved from port to port. Elias and Meirion pointed out the inefficiencies in the system, quoting Lewis Morris's description of mid-eighteenth century coastwaiters as 'Two Fools, one Rogue, one Bully and one Numbskull.' 'Tidewaiters' were Custom officers that met ships arriving on the tide, and ensured the safe discharge of goods to the satisfaction of the authorities. These 'tidewaiters' were either 'tidesmen', placed aboard each ship to supervise unloading, or 'tide surveyors' who had their own boat to visit each ship as she reached port. Because of local ties, most such employees were brought from outside the locality, with many coming from England. They were disliked by locals and could not be effective, with no knowledge of the language.

At one time it was estimated that 500,000 pounds of tea was smuggled out of an annual consumption of 600,000 pounds, so a large fleet of fast cutters known as the Preventive Service, was established to deal with the loss of government revenues. The smugglers' ships were different from most coastal vessels, being light with taller masts. Being usually fore and aft-rigged, they could put on more (and larger) sail and usually outrun the Preventive Service cutters. They could sail closer to the wind, so were more manoeuvrable and able to sail into creeks, narrow bays and estuaries. They also had a shallower draft than the Customs' cutters, and were easy and cheap to build. Such ships would normally carry a crew of 2-4, but instead there could be 10 or more smugglers aboard to sail the ships better, unload goods quickly, or fight the law.

Smuggling vessels were all fore-and-aft rigged, with sails like today's yachts, and this rigging helped its rapid spread. Square-rigged ships, with square sails, need the wind coming from aft (behind), and cannot move across the wind or into it. Fore-and-aft rigged ships sail most quickly across the wind, being able to sail into the wind by 'tacking'. (The vessel sails across and slightly up-wind, then turns and heads diagonally in the opposite direction, but again slightly upwind, progressing in a zig-zag manner.) Unlike a square-rigged vessel, a smuggler's boat could progress against the wind, into a creek to discharge her cargo, and sail away on the same tide.

In the early 18th century smugglers' ship were usually simple luggers, or gaff-rigged luggers under 50 tons. A lugger's mast was positioned close to the bows, and a sail hung from a diagonal spar, fixed about a third of the way along to the mast. The gaff rig added a second triangular sail in front of the mast, and the spar that supported the lug sail was joined at one end to the mast. From the middle of the 18th century, larger ships were used, to sail faster and carry bigger cargoes. Government sloops by 1760 averaged around 50 tons, with a few carriage guns, so smugglers began building larger, faster vessels up to 80 tons, arming them with more carriage guns and also swivel guns. Wherries and cutters were the boats of choice, gaff-rigged but with an extra sail on a longer mast above the main lug-sail, and another one at the bows, attached to a spar (the bowsprit), that extended straight forward from the bows. This long bowsprit gave a cutter great speed, and at one time only revenue vessels were permitted to use this particular spar.

For maximum speed, smugglers' ships were carvel-built, i.e. each board of the hull lapped up against the adjacent one, giving very smooth lines to slip easily through the seas. However, revenue ships were often slower, clinker-built vessels, constructed with each board overlapping the one below, increasing the ship's resistance and making her slower. Smuggling vessels were extremely cheap to manufacture, made from fir, and a lost ship could be quickly replaced. Built in traditional English oak, the king's ships were not only expensive but heavy to manoeuvre and slower. Also Revenue sloop crews were often worse than the smugglers, with weak captains who were often poor seamen, and the other crew-members serving the king against their will.

Landowners and squires were appointed to local Crown offices, such as County Sheriffs and Justices of the Peace, and especially in rural areas often considered themselves outside the law. The road network was terrible, and coastal ships were often the easiest way to travel. In 1739 Thomas Pennant wrote

Nant Gwrtheyrn beach, a noted haunt of Llŷn smugglers

that it took six uncomfortable days to travel from Chester to London along rough roads, and across unsafe bridges. During the 1700s it was reported that the tax collected on legitimate imports scarcely paid the wages of the finance officers who were collecting it. It was a constant battle for the 'revenue men' as often local magistrates and sheriffs were on the side of the smugglers because of the high taxes being levied. Smugglers arrived in the night, having been assured by signals from shore that no Customs cutters or officials were in the area. The ship grounded, or lay at anchor close offshore, and there followed a highly organised operation unloading on to the backs of horses and carts, to be quickly transported and hidden. In less than an hour, the smugglers could be away.

John Jones was caught smuggling brandy, with the possibility of life imprisonment, but by the end of 1758 was released on condition that he served upon the preventive cutter *Pelham*, based at Beaumaris, Anglesey. He had written for mercy a year previously, and I have altered the spelling and added full stops to make his plea more readable. '*I do make so bold on you as write these few lines to you in hoping you will pity my Deplorable case and hard wanting in my close Confinement. I am suffering to the So Point of Poverty as you ever see a Man in your day, for any sort of crime. I hope Your Honour Great Goodness of his Majesty's Customs to Acquaint them of my Sad Condition as I am suffering Since the Sixteen day of April 1756. I am Very Willing to go any way as their Honour Pleases for me that I may have my Bread before I starve in Prison. Pray Consider what Difficulty is to be a bon [?] Short Allowance for One Week time Which I am ever since I came to Confinement with my poor Wife and Six unhelped Children. If the Honourable Commissioners Let me go to one of his Majesty's Ships of War or anywhere Else as the Honours be Pleased for me to go from my Close Confinement and hard Wanting of Bread. As God shall be my Judge when I Depart from this World, I do not know where I shall have any more Bread in here. I have not a bed to Lie on, Nor any kind of furniture But What I have Already Should to keep me Alive in Prison with my Poor unfortunate Children. My poor Children (such as are able to Walk) went about from Door to Door to beg a Morsel of Bread in Order to keep me Alive in Prison which I refrained, Till every farthing Consumed of what I got in the World. Sir I hope that you will not be Angry to me to Explain the Truth, before you of my Condition as I am in I hope the Government Does not Order me to be Starve. There is [not] any Short of Allowance for Any One But what I can find myself, and that is nothing at Present. Sir, I have Petitioned the Honourable Commissioners for my Redemption from my Said Confinement but never heard no word ever since. I am sure if the Honourable Commissioners know of my Extremity and Miserable Condition as I am in, I am Sure if there any Christianity in them that they will Discharge me to some Way other to Labour for my Bread. If your*

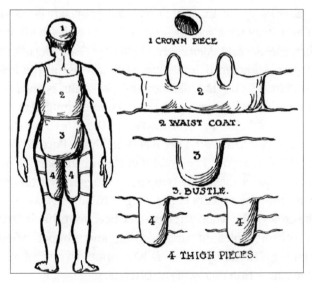

How Deal Boatmen smuggled tea ashore

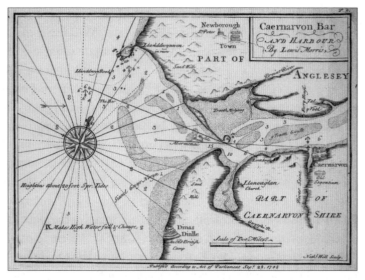

*Anglesey smugglers went to Ireland as passengers and hired
Irish Wherries to return with illicit cargo*

*Honour be Pleased to Acquaint them, I shall be in Duty Bound [and]
shall ever pray with you, as long as I live. – All from my poor
Unfortunate Servant, John Jones, Carnarvon Goal, Aug 9th 1757.'*

It is not known if Jones was still serving on the *Pelham*
when Platt tells us that 'Skomer and Skokholm islands to the
south were used as smuggling depots, and smugglers led by
Jack the Bachelor at St David's to the north scuttled a
government ship at Port-Ysky Bay [Porthlysgi, Porthlisky, near
Porthclais] in 1770... The *Pelham* cutter, in the service of the
customs...was attacked by two large smuggling cutters and a
wherry, and, the officers being obliged to quit it, was boarded
by the crew of the wherry. It has since been found at St David's,
with several holes in the bottom, and almost rifled of
everything. The Commissioners have offered a reward of £200
for the conviction of any of the offenders.'

William Owen's activities often encompassed the Isle of

Man. From 1405-1738 the Isle of Man was controlled by the Stanley family, with Sir John Stanley in 1405 being given the title of King of Mann by Henry IV. The title King of Mann was replaced in 1521 by the title Lord of Mann, held today by the reigning British monarch. In Owen's time James Murray, 2nd Duke of Atholl (1690-1764), was Lord Privy Seal from 1724 and 'Lord of Mann' from 1715, and his correspondences in the *Atholl Archives* inform us of some of the problems caused by Owen. Ireland and the Isle of Man were conduits for much Welsh smuggling of 'luxury' goods, such as wines, spirits, silks and tobacco from Continental Europe. Not until Atholl's death did Man's lordship revert to the Crown, so from 1765 Man lost favour as a smugglers' haven. Up until 1765, as a private property, it was free of taxes, so was a wonderful conduit to smuggle goods to the western coasts of Britain. The English government was losing £750,000 a year (£91,000,000 today) in excise duties until this time. Man was not officially part of Britain, so goods would be brought into Ireland and Man from the Americas and Continent, and stored there without any fear of discovery by Customs. Brandy, tea, sugar, salt and soap were stockpiled and brought over the Celtic Sea when the price was right. (Man never became part of the Kingdom of Great Britain or the United Kingdom, and is a self-governing Crown dependency). It is against this background that William Owen operated along the coasts of England, Wales, Man, Ireland and Scotland, and perhaps privateered across the Caribbean.

Constantly increasing excise duties (basically taxes) were used for political as well as financial ends. Public safety and health, public morals, environmental protection, and national defence have all at times been justifications for the imposition of an excise. For instance, in defence of excises upon strong drink, in 1811 Adam Smith wrote: 'It has for some time past been the policy of Great Britain to discourage the consumption of spirituous liquors, on account of their supposed tendency to ruin the health and to corrupt the morals of the common people.' Smith somewhat agreed with the tax, as it raised considerable revenues from more expensive drinks, while he praised the wholesome qualities of 'invigorating' beer and ale. Charles Lamb (1775-1834) again took the view of the vast majority of the population when he wrote (under his pseudonym Elia): 'I like a smuggler, he's the only honest thief. He robs nothing but the Revenue – an abstraction I never greatly cared about. I could go out with them in their mackerel boats, or about their less ostensible business, with some satisfaction.' (– *Elia and the Last Essays of Elia*, 1833).

Footnote 1 – The Importance of the Isle of Man to Owen

The Isle of Man was beyond the jurisdiction of the British Treasury, with its first Crown officials being appointed in 1682, but encountering opposition. Local customs duties, levied on behalf of the 'Lord of Mann', were minimal compared to those on the mainland, and Man's location made it an ideal entrepôt for smuggling. Legitimate traders had used the warehousing facilities at Douglas, Peel, Ramsey and Port Erin to avoid the costs of storage on the mainland and associated interest charges, when payment of duties had to await disposal of

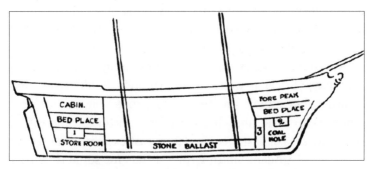

A smuggling schooner with 1, 2 and 3 being hiding places

cargoes. The huge profits to be made from smuggling cheap alcohol and other 'luxury goods' attracted 'Broken Merchants and others of Desperate or Low Fortunes' to Man, and smuggling became a huge industry. Attempts to check the movements of ships and their cargoes from Man were resisted by communities whose livelihoods depended upon the

Men carrying staves, known as batsmen, often assisted and defended the landing of contraband

island retaining its privileges. Officers installed by the Board of Customs feared arrest if they attempted to search ships in Manx ports, and generally could only observe, also being sometimes unable to report back when there were smuggling vessels sailing to England. However, the Duke of Atholl had to take care not to overly upset the British government, and possibly lose his lucrative personal customs incomes, which is why he became so concerned with the murderous smuggler William Owen, who had killed Customs Officers on the mainland.

At this time, Great Britain and Ireland monopolized the trade of alcohol and spices (the latter via the East India Company) and stopped independent shipments from abroad.

Man was generally free of taxes and boundaries of trade and it quickly became the centre of Britain's bootleggers. With taxes high, the opportunism of Manx smugglers for three centuries allowed Irish and Continental goods to be shipped to the mainland. The supply of tobacco to Man came 'chiefly from Dunkirk' possibly costing a loss in revenue to the Crown of £200,000 per annum. It was noted that 'The contraband trade from the Isle of Man is carried on almost entirely by wherries built at Rush' [16 miles from Dublin], with several having been 'purchased by the Isle of Man smugglers for the purpose of running goods on the coast of Scotland. Within a few years they have increased the dimensions of their wherries, that although they are quite open boats they have sailed round the north coast, and have landed their cargoes in the most western parts of this kingdom.' In Owen's time there were 'nine or ten large wherries, and above twenty boats in the Island, constantly employed in the smuggling trade.' Owen found it more profitable to smuggle into the north-west of England, with its larger centres of population, and 'runs on the Lancashire and Cumbrian coasts were so numerous it was reckoned the preventive men would have needed to have lined the shore, each man in sight of the next, before the landings would be reduced.' With the consent and assistance of most people in Man and the United Kingdom, the nature of the sparsely populated coastline with over a thousand landing places, and an under-resourced Customs service, smuggling was a relatively easy and attractive 'career' for William Owen.

Footnote 2 – GLAMORGAN SMUGGLING 1712–1785

The following records demonstrate the problems of policing smuggling, even along a less isolated coast, like that of Glamorganshire.

Custom House Records: Order Book, 1686–1733, Cardiff Records: volume 2 (1900) reports are as follows:

1712. A French vessel laden with wine and brandy ran ashore at Sully, and her cargo was seized by the Customs officers. The country folk assembled with guns & pistols, and endeavoured to take the brandy. Whereupon Mr Morgan, the Comptroller of Cardiff, went with some of his officers and some dependents of the Lady of the Manor of Sully, and dispersed the mob.

1732. Cardiff Custom officials wrote to the Admiralty Board in London (5 February 1732), informing them "the Smuglers do begin in this Channel to appear already, and about a fortnight ago there was one of them, of Aberthaw & Barry, but no Boat did Venter out to her, the prosecution against Butler and Walters having so much alarm'd them." They asked the Board to station a small sloop in the Bristol Channel, "built plain, without any painting or ornament, nor any Colours to be put out." They believed that all smugglers "would be afraid of every sloop they saw, that came near to her burthen, when she is so disguised." The *Hawk* Revenue Sloop, Captain Hawshaw, was appointed in 1732 to cruise between Milford and Bristol's King Road harbour.

1734. Cardiff officials reported to the Board: "At Aberthaw and Barry, when any boats goes out to em from thence, the Owners of em have always a Spye on the officer; and when they find him of one side of the River at Aberthaw, they'll land what they have of the other; and by reason there's no Boat in the Service, nor any boat on those accounts to be had for love or money, and the Officer obliged to go to a bridge about two Miles round, they have time enough to secure the goods before he can get there. Nay, there is instances that they have run'd goods in the day time before the officers face in this Manner. At Barry tis the same case; if they find the officer on the Iseland they'll land the other Side of the Harbour. If the other Side of the Harbour, they'll land on the Iseland, and the officers can't get over till the Tide is out, which may be five or six hours; and there is so much Cover on the Iseland, and such conveniencys for hiding of goods the other side, that an Officer has but a poor Chance to meet with em after they are landed. At Ogmore River it is the same case, and so at Aberavon." The Admiralty responded that the sloop Severn, stationed at Portishead, was enough to prevent smuggling in the Bristol Channel, but Cardiff officials wrote back asking for an Revenue cruiser.

1735. Rum was seized at Aberthaw. The officer saw a small boat go out of the harbour to a ship going up Channel. About noon the boat returned, Richard Forest came on shore very drunk, with Thomas Sweet the boat owner. George Robins stayed on board to keep the boat offshore, so that the excise officer could not board. Sweet told the officer that Robins wished to have a little fun with him, and that he had a few bottles of rum on board. The officer borrowed a boat and made for Robins, but the he escaped sailing towards Barry. After nightfall, officers on shore saw Sweet and Robins bring the boat back into Aberthaw harbour, and a person come ashore with a cask on his back. The excise officer gave chase on horseback; and on the smugglers' being overtaken, one of their party, Thomas John, used a stone to cave in the cask, destroying evidence.

1737. Cardiff officials wrote to London, denying a report that great quantities of tea and other goods are daily run along the coastline. They stated that since the Act of Indemnity, smugglers made no attempt in their district. The *Pye* snow (Charles Adlam master), and the brig *Priscilla* (John Longland master), both bound with tobacco from Virginia for Bristol, were wrecked at Nash Point near Southerndown. There was major difficulty in keeping "the country" from pillaging the wreck. A merchant, Mr Chamberlain, went to the scene, and discovered the hogsheads were all damaged, but and local people had hoisted some of the cargo up the cliff with ropes. Mr Chamberlain wanted it thrown into the sea, in the interests of the merchants and the Revenue. The 'mob' refused point-blank, not only stealing the damaged hogsheads despite the presence of excise officers, but even burning the hull to salvage its iron. Three or four hundred people assembled at the site every night 'from all parts of the Country towards the Hills; p'ticularly from a place calld Bridgend, from whence came a Gang of Ruffians the last day the Proclamation was read.' There were no soldiers stationed anywhere near to deal with the locals.

1787. The custom book records "It was thought absolutely necessary on the Death of Charles Bassett, to put a Person at Aberthaw immediately; for if that place had been left open, it would have been fill'd with Smugglers." There is no more smuggling tobacco carried on by vessels here now; "that Trade was totally put a stop to by our driving that Notorious Smugler Knight from the Island of Barry. When his armed Vessel was there, he was in such Force that it was impossible to approach the Island."

1788. Edmund Traherne, the Cardiff Collector sent to London an account of two expeditions against the noted smuggler Arthur, and asked them to station another cutter at Penarth; "but we are confident that Sixty Men of light Infantry are likewise wanted. How can the People of Neath and Swansey face Arthur without some such Assistance? And as in all probability the Island of Barry will be again inhabited by Smuglers, we shall not be able to approach the Place without Soldiers."

Glamorgan, like all Welsh coastal counties, had dozens of hidden landing places

The people of the "The Island of Barry, the Fortress of Knight the Notorious Smugler", led by William Doggett, illtreated Alexander Wilson and Evan Thomas, the Deputy Comptroller & Surveyor.

1769. In February the French snow *La Concorde*, out of Calais (Dominique Berthe master), of 140 tons burden, began to capsize off Aberthaw. The crew made shore in the ship's boat, but the *La Concorde* drifted west and was stranded on rocks off Saint Donat's Castle. It was reported "The Country People as soon as ever the Tide left her according to the savage Inhuman and Detestable Custom of the Country fell upon her and before I cd get together the officers belonging to the Port and arrive at the Place, it being almost Twenty Miles Distant, at least two thousand People with Hatchets were at work on her cutting and destroying everything they met with and carrying off the

Brandy and wine in small casks a great Part of which they spilt in the general hurry and confusion which must ever attend a scene of such Rapacity and Devastation. I exerted myself as much as possible at the hazard of my Life and the officers that attended me indeavoring to Prevent them but to no purpose. The Justices that attended were equally unsuccessful. The Country People by taking lights on Board to work in the night set her on Fire by which she was intirely destroy'd." County Justices met at Cowbridge to issue warrants against four persons. One was taken, but the constables allowed him to escape. A threatening letter was sent to the Cardiff Collector about his proceedings in the affair, and he asked to be allowed to purchase two brace of pistols and sidearms. He later reported to London that "The Teloscope was bought without any order, but is thought very necessary, as we can see every Vessel that goes to the Flat Holmes an Island where Smugglers at present run a great deal of Goods, and cannot just now be prevented by us as our Boat is too Old to go into any Sea."

1784. Upon 3 April wine was seized on Barry Island. "Thomas Knight a Noted Smuggler who resides a great Part of his Time on the said Island," told Thomas Hopkins, Waiter and Searcher at Barry and Sully, that the wine should remain there; "which Wine on entering the House a Second Time was all removed from thence... The said Knight carries on a very Considerable Trade in the Smuggling Way, and is so strongly supported, that there are but particular Times that I can venture to send my Officers to the said Island, he has sometimes I am informed 60 or 70 Men with him from on Board a large Cutter on the Smuggling Trade, which we suppose Knight to be the Proprietor of." Upon 17 April smugglers were again active: "A large Cutter is now off the Island of Barry of 24 Guns and 35 Men running Goods on the said Island." Upon 18 November officials wrote to London about seizure of tobacco. "it's with great Truth we assure you that the People here are in such Dread of Knight and his Gang, that we found a difficulty in finding People to Work for us."

1785. A letter repeated the problem "Herewith we return you Griffins Petition relative to his Boat seized at Knights Island of Barry... and beg leave to remark beside, that we can't conceive any body has any Business there, who is not connected with Knight in Smugling."

Chapter 2

William Owen's Death Cell Confession

[I have added paragraphs, amended the spelling, truncated over-long sentences and generally taken out capitals within sentences, to make Owen's story more readable. Where I have noted explanatory additions, they are enclosed in square brackets. Owen's life is recounted in the third person, and may well have been written in Owen's cell by the Reverend John Davies. Alternatively, Davies may have amended the 'confession' for moral purposes.]

Inscription on inside cover: *Daniel G. Matthias' Book 12th January 1811*

The Birth, Life, Education and Transactions of Captn. William Owen, the Noted Smuggler Who was executed for the murder of James Lilly at Carmarthen on Saturday the 2nd day of May 1747 Written by his own hand when under Confinement, and delivered to Mr Daniel James of Carmarthen aforesaid [the county gaoler] in the presence of Mr John Davies the clergyman, who attended him a few days before his execution. A True and Authentic Account of the Life of Captn. Wm. Owen

William Owen was born in the Parish of Nevern, in the County of Pembroke, South Wales, of a very honest and creditable family, his father being looked upon as the most substantial farmer in the said Parish; the said William Owen being his only son was a great favourite, particularly of the mother, his father

Nevern Church, where Owen would have been baptised

bringing him up with the best education that the country could afford. However, finding his son had no taste for the farming business, his father often recommended to him what way of life William would choose, and proposed that he would give William further education. He suggested William was to be sent to university to be a clergyman, or that he would bind him as an apprentice to an attorney. These proposals William rejected, and often told his father he was instead going to sea. It was very remarkable, that when he was then fighting not with his equals, but with those who were older and bigger, that he most commonly got the better of them, by some stratagem or another. He often applied to his father to have the art of navigation taught him, but his father was resolved to make a scholar of him, so he would not comply with William's request.

One morning William was going to school, the school being some way from the house. He had a little horse he used to ride, and instead of going to school, he rode away to Haverfordwest.

There, he bound himself as an apprentice to go to sea, in a small vessel of about 40 tons, which followed the Bristol Trade. He stayed on board that vessel for twelve months, then took his leave without bidding his master *adieu*. William was tired of such slavery as cooking the kettle, and receiving a few strokes with the rope-end now and then, thought himself too much of a gentleman to put up with such rough usage.

He returned to his father, who received him with great joy. After William was home a little while, his father wished him to help in his farming business, and set him to working, such as holding the plough, threshing and reaping and the like. His father used to tell him, that as William had not chosen to accept his offer of taking up any trade or calling, and had chosen a profession of his own accord and fled from that, that he wished his son to take over the business of farming from him. He desired William to work as he himself had done before, and said that the bread he got by the sweat of his eye-brows was the best bread he could eat. William would answer, that he would act as his father's steward, and see after the servants, to ensure that they did their business. His father answered that he could not afford to keep stewards.

William always possessed a hot, proud spirit, and asked 'Must I put myself on a level with the common labourers?' Being displeased, he left his parents and went aboard a Bideford vessel, where he continued for some time. Being very well respected, he was given half a man's wages. His father, having discovered that his son had left home a second time, greatly lamented that he had put him to work, and his wife gave him little ease for so doing. At last, William took flight and returned home to see his friends, being pretty well provided with money and clothes, but at the time had no thoughts of staying. There was great joy to see him, especially in such good order. William then being sixteen years old, his parents prevailed upon him to stay, promising him a small vessel. This idea he liked exceedingly well. [If we take a birth date of 1717, this would be 1733].

When his parents had bought the vessel, William took to debauchery and kept company with Madam Stokes' maid of Cardigan, to whom he pretended love, and grieved his parents. [John Stokes was a Cardigan solicitor who later also practised at Haverfordwest. He also features in the tale of James Lilly, murdered by William in 1747]. William was at that time [1735] only eighteen years old. His father, seeing him carrying on in such a wicked and lewd way, resolved to take his vessel off William. He told his son that he would make over all he had to his sister, who was more deserving. Then out of revenge William Owen married his lady's maid, and her friends promised to buy him a vessel. [He married Anne Nicholas at Cardigan on 15 February 1735.] However, he soon found out his mistake, for he had no fortune with her. His father, seeing his son had married one of little means, in pity received William back into his favour. He returned William's boat to him as a free gift, and likewise a sum of money to begin trading. William continued trading up and down the coast for one whole year. He then resolved to make a voyage to the Isle of Man, for a cargo of tun goods, in order as he thought, to increase his fortune. [Tun goods were mainly composed of barrels and casks, often containing wine or spirits, which were extremely heavily taxed and therefore popular items for smuggling]. But when he returned, he had all his venture [goods] and vessel seized by the Customs House officers. By this time his wife had borne him a daughter, and he reflected that these misfortunes had come from marrying so soon. [Ann Owen was baptised on 9 November 1735].

At last William Owen resolved to go abroad to seek new adventures, sailing out of Bristol for the West Indies, as second mate on a ship called the *Joy*. Having some cross words with his captain during the passage, he struck him. When they arrived in Barbados, and the ship was moored, William got his chest and bedding from below decks, and threw them into a small boat called moses that lay alongside. [This tells us that William was in the West Indies. In the Caribbean a 'moses boat' was a kind of broad flat-bottomed boat used especially for fishing, or to transfer goods and passengers between ship and shore.] William came to the captain and offered him a glove inviting a duel. He said that he expected to see him next morning, upon such a hill at 9 o'clock, and to provide himself with a case of pistols and a sword, in order to give satisfaction for the abuse the captain undeservedly gave him at sea. William then jumped into the moses boat, and bade the men to put off. He drew his scimitar and said that if they would not, he would run them through. They put off, and he went ashore. The next morning Owen went up the hill, borrowing a small sword, but not telling for what it was to be used. Immediately he saw the captain coming, Owen began to strip for action, thinking of nothing but the duel. [It appears that the case of two pistols was for each to fire one shot, and if there was no result, to take to swordplay].

However, soon there appeared a dozen men, constables and others, to take him for leaving his vessel [i.e. deserting, a crime]. Owen then trusted to his heels, and made off. After that, he shipped himself as mate on a ship called the *Terrible*, which was going to trade on the Spanish Main. She was mounted with twelve carriage guns and twelve swivel cannon. Her crew was twenty-five white men, thirty-five blacks and four boys, in all sixty men. They were obliged to be well-armed, as their trade was clandestine. In the year 1736, they lay at Carlisle Bay in Barbados. [This is the main harbour, adjoining the capital Bridgetown]. Owen was ever exercising and quartering the men, and greatly satisfied with his station. His taste was for honour by the sword. A proud, spirited man, he often projected how to blow the enemy up with gunpowder in casks, slung over the quarter-deck and other parts of the vessel, in case the enemy should attempt to board her.

This project pleased Owen, and was greatly approved of. By fixing loose stanchions [posts or bars] over the sides of the vessel with single blocks, reeved [threaded through rings] with a single rope, he could run out the casks in a moment. The casks that held the powder for that use were iron, with a fuse in each cask. His method in firing was by placing an overly long red-hot iron rod, to be put out through a loop-hole, to light the fuse in the powder casks, which could then be run out onto the enemy's deck. However, his captain used to check him, and said that 'his projects should not take place any longer.'

Owen then went to the merchants and told them that he was putting the vessel in the best posture for a defence, in case they should be attacked by the Spaniards, and that it was his captain had stopped him from so doing. The merchants went on board and saw what was done by Owen, and greatly approved of his schemes. They thanked him for his care and conduct, and made him a present of a black boy as an encouragement. They severely reprimanded the captain for being backward in his duty, as they might face an enemy. In trading, they had an exceeding fine price for their black slaves and other European commodities. Their way of trading was by night with the country people, standing off to sea by day. After they had sold their cargo, they took in a cargo of Spanish goods, and were bearing to windward in the morning. At sunrise they saw two sail to windward bearing right down upon them, upon which sight they got everything in readiness to engage, believing that they were two Spanish 'guard a coasters' coming to take them. [Owen's spelling for *guardacostas*, heavily armed and well-manned privateers protecting Spanish settlements and shipping. Smugglers cost the Spanish authorities vast incomes from taxes in their colonies in the New World. Spanish, French and English colonies generally all tried to avoid taxes imposed by their distant governments, and English, Dutch or French 'interlopers', or smugglers, would happily trade with enemy colonies].

The captain, being of a cowardly nature, wished to run away for Surinam [a coastal Dutch settlement now called Suriname, between Guyana and French Guiana], but Owen opposed his proposal and said that 'It was not consistent with power and glory, nor the interests of their merchants, nor their aim to go to Surinam, by reason of the great duties they would be obliged to pay, and it would ruin their voyage. For these reasons', said Owen, 'I do insist as a second man in authority aboard this vessel, upon a Council of War.' It was put to the majority of voices among the officers. The second mate, boatswain and gunner (being British men), loved Owen as their soul. The second mate was Owen's countryman, one 'John Thomas of Carmarthenshire', and they used to call each other 'Brother Will' and 'Brother John'. The boatswain, Owen and the gunner all styled one another 'Sincere Cousins'. Owen seldom conversed with the captain, only at mealtimes, but always talked with his countrymen, which occasioned the captain to be very jealous of Owen, but still he paid him all the homage due to a commander. A Council of War was held, and they all agreed to fight. Only the captain did not concur. Owen spoke for all the rest, and said to the captain, 'Sir, I am a Welshman, the honour my country gained in former times by their labour and courage. I am determined it shall not be backward in my days, to show the same labour as my forefathers did before me. I am, sir, to acquaint you that my brother officers and I have agree to fight them, if they prove to be Spaniards. You are to take your choice. Take the art of sailing upon you in the engagement, or retire to your cabin.'

The captain answered that he would sail the ship, then said 'Owen, I will go to my station and make all ready.' Owen being but a young man, and his countryman John Thomas an old trader, he consulted 'Brother John' about everything, the Spaniards being close at hand and seemingly preparing for boarding. Owen got his gunpowder casks ready to run out, and seemed to turn away from the approaching Spaniards. They came with Spanish colours flying, drums beating and trumpets sounding, as if they would devour them all at once. Owen hid all their guns, excepting only six swivels, and just twelve crew were on deck in order to decoy the Spaniards. They came alongside, one ship on the starboard quarter [right-hand stern], and the other on the larboard [port] bow, thinking that they could see no resistance, seeing neither men nor guns. They soon found their mistake, sending sixty men to board the *Terrible*, swords in hand. Owen ran out his gunpowder casks, and in a moment blew up twenty-five of them, and set the ship on the starboard quarter on fire. Then he fired a broadside and several volleys of small arms, which cost the Spaniards upwards of sixty men. They steered off in great confusion, repaired their damage in the best manner they could, and came up the second time, one alongside of the other, and engaged Owen's ship for around two hours. John Thomas was shot in the middle by chain shot, which killed him on the spot. Then the Spaniards, finding they could not gain the upper hand, made for the land.

Owen's ship was almost shattered, and they repaired the damage as best they could, making way for [English-held] Barbados. Owen had a very severe wound, caused by a musket ball in the back of his head. During the action, the captain had fled from his station to his quarters, and Owen had ordered the boatswain to sail the vessel. The Spaniards had killed seven black crew, four white men, and ten were wounded. Owen, by the consent of the boatswain, confined the captain to his cabin. They arrived in Barbados to the great joy of the merchants, where they called Owen as if he were a little prince.

Then Owen gave himself up to women, embracing all opportunities, being Conqueror over their sex. He went to a 'Pushing School' [brothel], and there he continued till the best part of his money had gone. Then he desired new adventures and went about in a fine ship belonging to New York and Barbados, called the *Mayflower*. Sailing for the Bay of Honduras, he had the fighting command. They arrived in the bay, and took in their cargo. Coming out, they were attacked by two Spanish 'Row Galleys', and after a three-hour engagement the Spaniards sheared off. They returned safely to Barbados, but the *Mayflower* was leaking badly. The men and officers behaved exceedingly well in the battle, with six killed and ten wounded. When they arrived in Barbados, they were very welcome guests of its merchants. Owen was still mightily well respected by all the neighbourhood, and looked upon as a sober, sensible, well-behaved man, not given to cursing nor swearing.

The only fault they had against him was his following lewd women – he had several with children of all colours. If a friend would advise him to take leave off that vile branch of sin, he would never again go to their house, so they resolved to let him go on in his own way, and would not affront him, as they had great respect for his valour and conduct. His next expedition was to Salamanca, an island belonging to the Spaniards, close by the Main, where the finest salt in the world is. [The Isla de Salamanca is off Colombia, where the River Magdalena meets the Caribbean]. The Spaniard does not live on it because there is no water. Owen was sent there to purchase a cargo of salt by force of arms, he being made captain of a schooner called the *Fly*. She carried six carriage guns, ten swivels and thirty-five men. Owen landed ten men in the night, and directed them to wheel the salt down that night to such a spot of ground, and to hide themselves in the day, for fear of being spotted from the Main.

The next night he sailed in, loaded the salt next morning and made sail, taking his departure for Barbados the next day. Seven leagues N.N.E. of Salamanca, William Owen met a Spanish *guardacosta*. She carried ten carriage guns, fourteen swivels and seventy-five men, and they engaged in battle for two-and-a-half hours, then the Spaniard bore away from him. Owen lost three blacks and one white man, with five wounded. [Many blacks worked as free men on privateers and merchant ships in the Caribbean. At one time the greatest pirate of all time, Black Bart Roberts, had over 80 blacks sailing with him, of equal status with white crew]. Owen arrived safe at Barbados, where they still increased their love for him.

After he had been there a while, he was asked to go to [French] Martinique in the same vessel, to take on a cargo of goods at a creek near Fort St. Philip's, and to smuggle that cargo to Willoughby Bay on the island of Antigua. He was told that they had a pilot ready for him, and that all he had to do was to go to each place, and boats would come out, load and discharge his cargo. This he did accordingly, and made a profitable voyage for the merchants. His next voyage was to sail again for Martinique for a cargo of French goods, to be smuggled back to Barbados. As he was approaching Barbados, one of our fifty-gun ships, the *Oxford*, stationed at Barbados, being to windward, came to gunshot range of Owen. The man-of-war then fired several shots at him, but he would not come to, thinking to gain the windward of her. However, a chain shot carried away the head of his main mast, six foot under the crowns. [This plural could be an abbreviation for the crow's nest, or may simply refer to the top of the mast]. This caused poor Owen to strike his colours. He was brought on board the man-of-war, and the captain took him by the hand, and said 'Owen, is it you I have taken? You are a brave young fellow, and I will use you as such.' He answered the captain, saying 'Sir, I know it was your honour that chased me, otherwise I would have thrown my cargo overboard to save my vessel.'

The captain replied, 'Do you say so, Owen? I will then, upon my honour give to the owners their vessel, and you your venture and wages.' The captain told him that he must stay aboard and that he would be his sincere friend, and he would promote him as soon as possible. Owen was to act as a midshipman and was to be treated as such. Owen continued aboard the man-of-war for twenty months. The captain made very free with him, dining once a week with Owen, who often had the honour of going ashore as the captain's companion. Owen now received a letter from Europe from his father, which came by way of London (and had the Post Office stamp upon it). [This was a general Royal Mail stamped impression, as postage stamps had not been invented]. The letter acquainted Owen that his wife had borne him a son as well as his daughter, since he left the country. His wife now lived very well in Cardigan town. Owen took this very much to heart, and wished he was with them, being then master of a considerable amount of money. Owen managed it so well as to forge a letter, the contents of which explained that his uncle was dead, and had left him an estate of two-hundred pounds a year, and a thousand pounds in cash, as well as livestock and crops, he only paying two-hundred and fifty pounds legacy.

Owen now petitioned the captain for a discharge. The captain sent for him, and perusing the letter immediately gave Owen his discharge, wishing him much joy. The captain asked him the name of his new family seat, saying he 'would come and pay him a visit if ever he should happen to come to those parts.' Owen answered that his estate was named Tre-minvow (a large mountain, so-called in Pembrokeshire). [No such place seems to exist – it seems to be a corruption of *Tremaenfawr*, Place of the Great Standing Stone. Equally, he could be alluding to an actual place. Tremaenhir is a Grade II listed farmhouse near the port of Solva, Llanhowell and Llandeloy, Pembrokeshire. It is situated between two standing stones, one called *Maen Hir*. *Maen Hir* means long stone, and is generally used to denote a standing stone (a menhir), and *tre* signifies place. There is another fallen stone nearby, and the tre might also signify three standing stones.] He soon set out on his voyage to England, taking his leave of the merchants, promising to return if things did not answer his needs at home.

He arrived at Portsmouth in November, after an absence of three-and-a-half years, clothed himself suitably for the climate, and came to Wales by way of [sailing from] Bristol. He was kindly received by his friends, and especially by his father and mother, who had grieved much after he had gone abroad, contrary to their inclinations. His father, finding that William

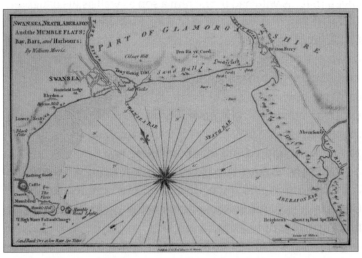

Swansea, where Owen purchased the Dispatch *in Autumn 1739*

had made good use of his time, resolved to give him a sum of money, in order to enable him to buy a good vessel. Owen went to Swansea, bought a ship and called her *Dispatch*. As he was going through Carmarthen town, a fatherless and motherless boy named William Lewis approached him and asked if he wanted an apprentice. Owen told him he would take him on trial, and came to greatly approve of the boy, and bound him for five years. Owen and William Lewis went with this vessel, and followed the Bristol trade, in which Owen was so expeditious that he made two voyages in autumn in three weeks' time from Cardigan, and got eighty pounds clear gain from these two voyages [over £12,000 today].

His wife disclosed to him that she had a liaison with a gentleman in his absence, which made him turn away from his love, so that he hated her as if she was a devil, but he kept all this very close to himself, to prevent such reflections as being called a cuckold. [His son could not have been his, being conceived in his long absence]. He then gave himself up to debauchery out of lust and revenge, but still was very expeditious in his voyages, and kept such thoughts hidden from the world. He took a house and storehouse in Cardigan town, in order to cure herrings, and follow malting, with other branches of trade. Success greatly attended him, and as trading increased, so did he himself in pride and luxury, but still he looked upon his wife as no more than a servant maid. In short, he kept her in a handsome manner in the eyes of the world, but she had no command of cash. He would often send her out of town upon a sham errand, that he might have the better opportunity of enjoying others. He would often think of turning her out, but he considered the inconvenience of it, by receiving the ill-will of his friends in so doing.

Owen agreed in 1740 to go on a voyage to Dublin, freighted by one James Lilly, with a cargo of barley. [In 1742 Owen bought an action against Lilly, presumably for non-payment of this freight shipment to Dublin in 1740, and in 1747 shot him]. Owen was detained there for a considerable time under an embargo [a ban on trade], and there took a great liking to a very beautiful woman. By laying several stratagems, in a little time he had the pleasure of drinking tea with her. Then with the interest of another he had bribed, there was a correspondence settled. He then had opportunity to command, being greatly affected by her beauty, her sweet voice in singing, and pleasant modest behaviour. She again, on the other hand, being well pleased with his conversation, his speech and fine stories, made her take a great fancy to him. After the question was put to her, she said that she 'would like him for a husband, more than any lord in the land.' He answered that if he was Emperor of Austria, only she would be made his Empress. Owen told her that he had made a voluntary oath, never to go before a clergyman upon any such occasion, for his word and protestation was sufficient for a marriage. With much ado, he prevailed at last, and went in a coach to the country, and pretended they were married, and lived together in a room while the embargo continued. But Owen found he had made a great mistake. Instead of a virtuous virgin, he had a mistress that a certain lord kept, who had got a fine boy by her. His lordship, living then in London, allowed forty pounds a year for her maintenance. This made William mad with himself, as he had a great veneration for her. He left Dublin, and went no more near his pretended wife, but soon after sold his vessel and bought another one that was bigger.

He then cut a great figure in the world, and was worth a large sum of money, being mightily well respected by gentlemen, and others with who he had any dealings. His father would often advise him to leave off his debauchery, but he would turn his back to his father and his advice, which occasioned great grief to his father. However, William Owen was very remarkable for being charitable and ready to help the distressed, and never cared much for pot [drinking] companions. Owen then began to follow the smuggling trade with great conduct and success, making several undiscovered trips. One time he was loading corn at Cardigan, and a mob of eighty or more persons arrived, stirred up by one in the neighbourhood with whom Owen had quarrelled. His vessel [the *Blessing*] was then in the River Teifi under Cardigan town, fully loaded, and the mob came to her by boats and began to rifle the cargo [on 1 March 1741]. Owen, with his two apprentice boys, rushed to their small boat and rowed up alongside.

Owen was provided with several small arms, and demanded their authority for rifling his vessel. The mob swore they would cut him to pieces. Owen spoke to them fairly, but the situation grew even worse, and he was forced to fire over their heads, but they only laughed at him. By this time they had broken open the hatches, unfurled the mainsail and put it into one of their boats.

Finding none of the mob would stop, Owen fired into them. The chief among them received a pistol ball in his spine, which wound was likely to prove mortal. Owen then entered the vessel on one side with sword and pistol in hand, and drove them all before him, overboard into their boats. They carried the mainsail with them. Owen, finding them landed, pursued after them, now about a hundred in number. They caught up with the mob, and made them carry the mainsail back to his vessel and ask pardon. It was very remarkable that the mob was so numerous and all living in one town, and had never been overcome before, making the very magistrates do what they wished. They did not take Owen for an enemy when they made their submission to him. He made a peace with them on condition they would tell him who put them up to the attack. They told him, and said that they had 'never thought of offending him, but had been made drunk.'

Sometime after that, Owen went to Waterford, a fine sea port in Ireland, with a cargo of pickled herrings, where he took a great liking to a gentlewoman who was a widow who kept a coffee house and tavern, which he frequented often. At last, as he had grown greatly in the lady's favour, she often came aboard his ship wearing a mask. He became so great a favourite that she could not bear his absence. But Owen noted her one time, concerned in liquor, and ever since he would not go near her, for he hated a drunken woman above everything. On that voyage Owen bought a large venture of tun goods for South Wales, and arrived at his intended place, called Coaltop Road in Saint Bride's Bay near Milford Haven. [A road, or roadstead, is a sheltered anchorage, and this must have been near one of the Pembrokeshire coal mines]. One night he had several gentlemen on board, and spotted a vessel very like a King's Cutter [a Revenue boat] coming into the roadstead. Owen told the gentlemen that she was coming to take him, and the gentlemen admitted that they wished to go ashore. Owen answered 'As you are gentlemen, I do expect you will show yourselves as such, by taking hold of musket and firing on

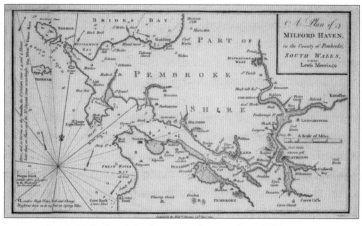

St Bride's Bay and Coal Top Roads were often used by Owen

behalf of the weaker side, who has everything at stake.' Then Owen fired a shot at the ship, and made it shear off. She proved to be another smuggler, which was loaded with salt. Owen had taken them to be a customs cruiser, and then they had thought the same of him.

He decided to rebuild his vessel, and built her in the form of a warlike ship. Accordingly he made a fine vessel of her, and fitted her out as grand as a King's Yacht, calling her the *Prince Charles*. The first enterprise that Owen took, before he sailed with his newly built vessel, was against the Johnes's of Abermâd mansion, Llanfarian, near Aberystwyth, on behalf of Mr. Thomas Parry, an Aberystwyth gentleman. [Abermâd was rebuilt and is now known as Henblas, and was the residence of Thomas Johnes, High Sheriff from 1737 and imprisoned for debt in 1757. Parry brought an action against Johnes in 1741, and his house was attacked in retaliation upon 14 June 1742. Owen then claims to have led an attack on the High Sheriff's house in that year]. Parry was a very eminent lawyer, a man of very considerable estate, well beloved of all that ever had the pleasure to know him. He had disobliged these persons of Abermâd by demanding his own [money owed]. For that reason they were determined to do him some mischief, wherever they could find him. Mr. Parry was a very sincere friend of Owen's, and as Owen was always very grateful to his friends, he resolved to go to Mr. Parry's assistance. These Johnes's were always armed, and always had about forty people at Abermâd, and had four small cannon mounted on top of the house. Several gentlemen in Pembrokeshire, as well as Cardiganshire, took men to go to Mr. Parry's assistance, and nominated William Owen as their general. Owen, at the head of the men, marched that day to within four miles of the place, where he was joined by several gentlemen, and others.

Next morning, Owen got up very early and marched to

Abermâd, where he was to be joined by the gentlemen. He drew his men up on the side of a hill opposite the house, about half a mile away. He saw men in the house, and on top of it, well-manned and everything ready to receive his attack, upon the sight of which most of Owen's men began to tremble. Then Owen went among them, and viewed them all, and asked which ones were the brave fellows, who would stand by him to gain glory that day. Several declared that they would die by him that day. Owen responded, 'Do you say so, my brave fellows? And so will I by you. I am certain we shall conquer them.' When the gentlemen came up and joined him, the Knight of the Shire came to Owen, and said, 'General, what think you of this affair?' 'Sir', said Owen, 'I will make all speed I can to open the siege.'

Then Owen, at the head of them, marched towards the house, and took a great long way around to avoid coming under their cannon fire. When they were within a gunshot of the house, its defenders fired a whole volley at them. Several received slight wounds, and most of Owen's men began to run away. Finding out what sort of men he had, Owen armed a number of them, just those he could depend upon, to the number of eighteen men. Then he nominated proper officers, as follows: Thomas Morgan, major; David Jones, captain; John Owen, lieutenant; William Lewis, ensign [Owen's apprentice]; George Lloyd, sergeant; and Thomas Davies, corporal. Then General Owen gave the following speech to his officers and men, 'Gentlemen, we are come here to make a conquest over a parcel of lawless persons, who disturb the peace of our country, especially of our friend Mr. Thomas Parry, whose life they have so often threatened. Those people are disagreeable to God, and you, my worthy fellows, who I know have honour and bravery in you, set out with resolution and courage and attack them. Let every man act in his respective station, and mind to observe the word of command, so God bless our undertaking.'

They gave three huzzahs and marched with their general at their head, and every officer in his respective post. Owen drew them up, then reconnoitred the besieged, finding there was no possibility of coming close to the walls of the house, without bulwarks to shelter them from the besieged. So he got two wagons filled full with straw, and tied one cart to the other, and let them go with the slope of the ground, very close to the walls. They then opened the siege, which continued from eight in the morning till seven in the evening. By that time, Owen, his officers and most of his men were wounded. Ensign Lewis had a very dangerous wound in the head caused by a musket ball. At six in the evening Owen resolved to blow up the balcony to make a breach for an assault. For this purpose he put a cask of gunpowder in one of the wagons, set it on fire, ran it under the balcony, and then it blew up and did great damage. Then the besieged called for quarter and surrendered to the conqueror, having several on their side wounded. The gentlemen offered Owen a considerable sum of money, but his pride was so great, that he asked them if they took him to be a Swiss [a mercenary, a despised term].

The first voyage he took with his new vessel *Prince Charles* was to Waterford, with a cargo of herring in barrels, and he made a very good voyage. He took in freight for the Isle of Man, with the resolution to follow smuggling for some time. At the Isle of Man, he took in a large quantity of tea and sailed for Liverpool. When the customs officers came aboard at Liverpool, he dressed himself in a very grand manner, and dressed his men in livery. He told his men to tell the officers that he was a Welsh baronet, come pleasuring in his yacht, which the officers believed and did not open the hatches. Owen took care to land his goods that night. There he bought six swivel guns for his vessel, and plenty of small arms, powder and ball, double-headed shot and hand grenades. He returned to the island after six days absence, and made a fine voyage.

His next voyage was with tea and silk, and Owen landed near Milnthorpe [a village near Arnside] in Westmorland, where he used horses of an acquaintance of his, and packed up his goods in the form of Scotsman's pack, dressing himself in plaid like a Scotsman. [The Scotsman's Pack stands on one of the old trading tracks in Derbyshire. The inn was a regular calling place for food and shelter for the 'packmen' who visited every farm and village in the area offering their goods and carrying news. It gets its name from Scottish packmen who sold their tweeds there to local farmers.]

With two men and loaded horses, Owen set out from Milnthorpe and arrived at Liverpool [70 miles south]. No-one suspected Owen, thinking he was a pedlar, and he sold his goods in Liverpool at a good rate, returning to the island of Man after ten days absence. His next voyage was to Whitehaven with tea and silk, entering Whitehaven in the middle of the day. Passing for a gentleman who had come for pleasure, he sold his goods at a high rate, selling all but fifty pounds of tea. [Around this time the cost of tea veered between 7s 6d and 17s 6d per pound, around £57-£133 today. Loose tea costs around £10 a pound now]. One night he was at a well-wisher's house, who was a married woman, but Owen was her very favourite. They were in a room together tasting the tea, the landlady praising it as much to the taste of the ladies. Who should be in the next room, but two officers listening to them, but the landlady did not know them to be such. They had marked Owen by a spaniel dog that had followed him the other day. On Sunday the officers found Owen's vessel and about fourteen boarded her. [This happened in February 1743].

The surveyor told Owen that he had information against his vessel, and he must search her all over. 'Begin, then, with my cabin', said Owen, and they did so accordingly, then went to the hold where the forty pounds of tea was. Owen in the meantime was charging his small arms in the cabin [preparing his pistols for firing.] When they found the tea, and were bringing it on deck, Owen slipped his hawser [– a large rope or cable used for mooring, or towing a vessel], and went to sea with the officers and tea, and told them that the first who called for assistance was a dead man. A brisk wind blew, with a storm coming on, and the surveyor begged to be put ashore, offering Owen twenty pounds in money and the tea for so doing. Owen answered, 'Worthy sir, do not be afraid, I will not harm you. I do this for my own safety. This is all I have in the world, and if I lose this, I shall be a beggar.' He landed them at night about two miles from Whitehaven, having treated them exceedingly kindly, and sailed for Scotland.

The storm increasing, he forced his vessel against heavy seas until she was likely to sink, and the next morning he was forced to bear away before the wind for Workington, about five miles from Whitehaven. There he stayed for three days, and knowing how matters had proceeded at Whitehaven, was always on his guard.

The fourth day about thirty armed officers, and others, came upon him, his vessel being left dry by the ebbing tide. Owen called to them and asked them what they wanted, but they still advanced towards the vessel. Owen turned his swivel guns upon them, and made them stop, asking their business, being such a number, and armed, near his ship. They answered they were officers of the Revenue. Owen replied that he never knew men with firearms to be king's officers before, and made them keep away.

The king's cruiser [*Sincerity*] at Whitehaven had been double-manned on purpose to take Owen. Owen had intelligence of the cruiser being fitted out. Next morning it was pretty moderate, but a great sea on the tide. Owen got a distance of the sailors and boats and went to sea. Immediately he saw a sail bearing right upon him, and made her out to be the king's cruiser. His number of hands was then a stout man, two brave boys, and himself. Owen addressed his little crew, 'My brave boys, will you fight for your own liberty and property?' 'Dear master', they replied, 'we will die by you.' Owen responded, 'My boys, do not be too rash, look about, I'm sure we shall beat them. Do not be daunted by the number of their hands, or force, for the more in number they are, the surer we shall be of a shot among them. My lads, we have time enough, have a biscuit apiece and eat them, for you have not breakfasted, otherwise the smoke and fire will make you faint.' After they had eaten their biscuits, he gave each of them a glass of wine, and then drank his own glass of water, and said 'This water will show me courage!'

Then he began to put himself into a posture of defence by filling all his netting with spare sails, beds, oakum, etc. [By filling the netting, he raised the bulwarks, making it more difficult to board his vessel. Oakum is a mass of tarred fibres, often unpicked from old ropes, used for caulking or packing the joints of timbers in wooden vessels]. He had close quarters [wooden barriers] and stocks to shift all his guns to either side, he had blocks to shift upon the deck to prevent their boarding him, and in case they would board him on the bow, he would mount his swivel guns on these blocks on the quarter [rear] deck. He had a great number of fire arms (in short, his intent was all fire) – the like was never known in these seas. He filled his binnacle with powder, being resolved to blow up all, before he would surrender. The cruiser still chasing, and Owen having all in readiness, he ordered to lie to, for her to come up to him. Then she came pretty near to him, and he saw all on board under arms with drums beating.

Owen cried 'My boys, be not afraid of the noise of

parchment!' 'Not we', said the lads, 'they are a parcel of informing, perjured rogues. Their conscience makes them rue.' The cruiser fired her chase gun [a small cannon in the bow] at him, and Owen hoisted his colours, but they showed none. Owen did not think it proper to return another, then the cruiser fired again at him, and the shot almost took his head off. Owen had his crew sheltered by the netting, exposing none to their fire but himself. He then ran up alongside the cruiser, giving them three volleys in one minute's time. Owen gave three cheers and shot astern of her. The cruiser had eighteen men, six carriage guns and eight swivels. Owen tacked about, shifted his guns to the other side, upon her larboard quarter, and gave them three volleys again, shooting away their main runner and tackle gaff, mainstay, two of the fore shrouds, and their sails shattered to pieces. [The runner is the 'preventive backstay, or 'running backstay', which supports the mast from aft, usually from the quarter rather than the stern. When the boat is sailing downwind, the runner on the leeward side of the mainsail must be released so as not to interfere with the sail. Tackle is the term for the line, chains and hooks used with a block, and the gaff is the spar that is attached to the upper edge of a fore-and-aft mounted sail. While the other three crew members were sheltering, it is amazing that Owen could steer the ship and move heavy guns across the deck, load, prime and fire them, but the engagement actually occurred and the more powerful boat suffered real damage].

He then ran ahead of the cruiser, and he fired at them again now and then, their first courage being greatly abated. Owen sailed about again and came close under their lee, and gave them three volleys more, and threw on board two hand grenades and three powder flasks, which put the cruiser's men in great confusion (thinking the hand grenades to be devils) not seeing the like before. They all ran below the deck. [This

The official account of Owen's action against the Revenue Cutter off Workington 1 March 1743

part of the account is close to the truth].

Owen then hailed them, demanding that they strike their colours, and the captain came up to the deck and begged for his life. Owen told the captain that he was a pirate, and he would have them tried for piracy. The captain of the cruiser protested that he belonged to the Revenue. 'What!' said Owen, 'the Revenue is fitting out pirates?' The captain replied 'No, that is false'. The captain begged ten thousand pardons, and Owen told them to make sail, telling them he would advertise them [– probably as pirates]. The engagement was near the shore, and there were over three thousand eye-witnesses to the whole action, and all wished them well except the officers. Wishing to have sight of him ashore, that they might have known [?] him, the cruiser made for Cumberland, and Owen for Scotland, but the wind was against him so he sailed for the Isle of Man. A storm arose, and it blew very hard, so that night he was forced to the Ross Bay off Kirkcudbright, and the cruiser to

Whitehaven, in a shattered condition, to the great joy of all mariners. This happened on Thursday.

The cruiser was repaired, more men and guns put on board, and sent to sea on the following Saturday in order to take Owen, being satisfied by the weather that he must be at Kirkcudbright in Scotland. About twelve o'clock at night the cruiser sailed into Ross Bay, and came unawares in the dark alongside Owen, but he fired a gun and she moved further off. Next morning Owen brought his ship alongside the cruiser, with all his guns bearing on her, and commanded her captain to come aboard, asking him if he would deny coming sword in hand to board them. They all being terrified of Owen, the captain went aboard Owen's ship, where they kept him. Owen commanded the cruiser's men not to leave their vessel without his leave, on pain of their lives. Owen treated the captain of the cruiser very well, but still pretended that he believed the captain to be a pirate. Owen then commanded the cruiser's men to bring all their guns, as well as powder and ball, on board his ship, which Owen detained, along with the captain. The wind came fair, which was the 1st of March [1743 NS]. Owen returned their guns and captain, and ordered him to salute them with their thirteen guns as he sailed out of Ross Bay, which accordingly they did, agreeable to his order.

Next morning, he arrived at the Isle of Man, the news of the engagement arriving there before him. They received him with several cheers, hailed his vessel quite under the town, and caressed him as though he was their prince, which greatly agreed with Owen's pride and temper. He then fell greatly in love with a most beautiful young woman, of the family of the Kelly's of that country. She had a very good fortune, several very good houses in that town, and was then about eighteen years of age, but a man would not judge her to be above sixteen. She was very fair and exceedingly small in the waist. She had a promise of marriage to a young gentleman of quite a considerable fortune, but Owen, addressing her with fine speeches and his conversation being agreeable to her sex, soon turned him out of favour. Owen, by this time, could play exceedingly well on the German flute, the plain flute, small pipes and French horn, which added greatly to his interest in gaining the lady's favour, she being so engaged with Owen, that she doted upon him. Her friends were all against her having him, although they not knowing he had a wife in Wales, but all to no purpose. She did not mind her friends' advice. On the other hand, he doted on her, and, in short, never loved a woman before with such and affection.

Owen would grieve very much in himself to think that he was married, and would reason in himself whether vengeance would cry against him, or not. He considered that his wife had committed fornication, for which he was authorised by Scripture to divorce her, and that the law of the land empowered him to marry by applying to the House of Commons [– divorce had to be agreed by the Commons and was very expensive]. Yet, he considered the inconvenience, the aspersions of his adversaries, and the hurt the other woman might do him. His next expedition was to South Wales with a cargo of brandy, rum, claret, tobacco, silk and tea, and he parted with his new favourite and proceeded on his voyage. He arrived safe on the coast, where he met an Irish smuggler of force and ten men in a bay near Fishguard. This was one of Patrick Donohow's of Wexford's ships, with his pennants flying. Owen hoisted his pennant and ordered them to strike their colours.

They refused, so he fired a double-headed shot, so well-aimed that it carried away the head of their mast and pennant and they made no resistance at all. Then Owen directed his course for St. Bride's Bay. There he landed the most part of his cargo, and conveyed it to Haverfordwest. Some days after that, the same Irish smuggler came to the place where Owen's ship lay, Owen then being at Haverfordwest. The Irish captain [and some crew] tried to board Owen's ship, but the hands left aboard fended them off. The Irishman swore that as soon as his cargo was unloaded, he would take Owen (and his vessel) and skin him alive, then take his skin, and blow in it, and fit it for a buoy up on the anchor. Owen was returning the next morning and was intercepted by the Irish captain and three of his men at Little Haven. The captain attacked him three different times, but Owen beat him with pleasure. The crew finding their captain beaten, all fell upon Owen, seemingly with the resolution to murder him. However, some men came to his relief and saved him, but he was much wounded.

Owen then went on board his ship, and the Irish on theirs. Owen heaved up his anchor, determined to have satisfaction, came alongside them and was bent upon taking the Irish ship. He gave her a broadside, upon which the Irish captain cried for quarter. Owen boarded, and grappled his ship fast to their vessel. The Irish captain, upon his knees, begged for his life. Owen shouted at him 'You villain! Do you think I am as barbarous as you? No, my honour will not let me hurt you, as you have surrendered to me.' Owen took him on board as a prisoner. The Irish captain then had about half his cargo unsold. Owen ordered them to set sail and keep under his lee, and they stood off to sea together. There was one hundred pounds advertised for taking this Irishman, and he thought Owen was bent upon carrying him and his cargo to Cardigan. Owen made very much of him, made him dine with him, and drink plenty of wine and punch, and the Irish captain offered Owen forty pounds for his personal liberty. Owen said he would not take it, and the Irishman judged that Owen thought it was too little. He said 'I will give you eighty pounds, vessel and cargo.' Owen said 'No, I shall not take it. I will tell you what

I shall do. I shall give you your liberty, vessel and cargo for nothing, only behave well in the future to your betters, especially to me.' The Irishman fell on his knees, asking pardon for the abuse he gave Owen, that the heat of blood was over. Owen bade him to go on board his own vessel, and wished him well.

Owen then steered his course for Cardigan Bay, and when anchored there went to Cardigan town and went to his own house. He looked around him, and to his surprise found his wife dead drunk. He went to the neighbours where she frequented, and asked if she owed anything for ale. He found, that in his absence, she owed nearly ten pounds [almost £1,500 today] in four ale-houses. He paid them all off, and told them that if they ever gave his wife any further credit, he would never pay them. He tarried a while, then decided at all events to leave her, having the young woman on the Isle of Man.

The officers of the Revenue proposed to him to go cruising after the salt smugglers, who were very numerous along the coast, and Owen agreed with them to go accordingly, subject to certain conditions. He took two officers on board, and cruised up and down the coast until he had finished smuggling his own goods. He then went to the Isle of Man, where he arrived in good order, to the great joy and satisfaction of his own beloved. He then agreed to be married to this young woman, being resolved to go to some foreign parts to live, to prevent the aspersion of the world. She agreed to anything that was pleasing to him, but desired above all that he stopped smuggling, as he would do very well anyway.

Owen's next voyage was again to South Wales, where he arrived safely, carrying the same kind of goods as on the last voyage. He sold all immediately, some to Carmarthen, Laugharne, Haverfordwest & co, and arrived back at Man after eight days absence. He then resolved to take a trip to

Westmorland, where he had promised to come by at such a time, and took the young woman with him in order to be married, for they would not marry him on the island against her friends' consent as she was under age. They arrived between the broad sands on the borders of Westmorland, near the town of Grange-over-Sands. Owen set out for Kendal to his correspondent about the cargo, leaving charge of the vessel to a Yorkshireman he had aboard. He told him that they had put two officers in those parts, and when the ship lay dry, they would come down to board her, and he should secure them both in the forecastle. He was not to treat them ill, nor let them want for anything, only keep them safe until Owen returned the next day.

When Owen returned, he found his vessel taken. The Yorkshireman, instead of securing the two officers, had agreed to give up the ship for a sum of money. The officers had gone for assistance, and returned with about twenty armed men. This traitor sent all hands to sleep, telling them he would keep a look-out. He put all the great guns in the hold, and also chained Owen's fine dog there. When they came alongside, the rest of the hands heard them, got up and found an abundance of armed men. The lads took small arms to attack them, but this villain endeavoured all he could to hinder them. William Lewis came up with his piece, and shot his hand almost off, saying 'You are the villain that has ruined my master. I will be thy death.' The young woman was on board all this time, encouraging the lads to fight and handing the arms to them, but was overpowered, and the boys wounded and in a miserable condition. The victors made free plunder of everything, including Owen's four shirts, two pairs of stockings, and a suit of clothes, but the young woman preserved his papers and letters for him.

The poor boys, when bleeding on the deck, told them 'Give

us our master, we will fight you again.' They [the officers' men] had killed his fine dog that he had been offered fifteen pounds for. This put poor Owen at his wit's end. He was afraid to go near the place, to see how things stood, for fear of being taken. He went to Captain Frazer's house near Lancaster, and begged him to go and see how things were. The captain brought the young woman to Owen, along with the few things she had saved. They did not know where the boys had been taken, so made their escape. The affair cost Owen between four hundred and five hundred pounds [up to £75,000 today]. He asked the young woman if she thought less of him, by reason of his misfortunes. 'No', said she, 'keep your head up and I'll buy you a vessel.' Owen had only one shilling in his pocket, and the couple went on the road to Liverpool. Owen said 'All my concern is to part with you, without fulfilling our promises, by reason we have no money to spare.' Upon Owen's persuasion and solemn protestations to marry at the first opportunity, at last she came to agree his terms, to pass as man and wife and bed together. She set him as far as North Wales on his journey down to South Wales, then they parted.

She went to Liverpool in order to stay with her sister-in-law till he should return, which Owen said would be in five or six weeks' time. Then he came to Cardigan, made his loss known, and resolved to have a raffle for a cow. He went among the gentlemen of his acquaintance for that purpose, who subscribed half a guinea apiece towards the raffle. He got about thirty guineas for the raffle, settled his affairs in the best manner he could, then told his wife that he had resolved what he often before had told her, that he owned her no longer. As for the furniture, Owen said she could keep it, and gave her a guinea to pay the rent. He bought two horses, and rode away with his man William Lewis who had returned, heading for Liverpool, where he arrived to the great joy of his beloved. They both set out for the Isle of Man, being resolved to settle there for a while, Owen not finding himself in the condition of settling in a foreign part, according to his first intention. However, everyone in the island had it in their heads that he had another wife, but they bothered them little, as they honoured him for his good nature and bravery.

His first expedition was for Liverpool, with a venture of tea. He landed safely, a mile below the town in the night, making a good voyage and returning in five days. His next voyage was to Duddon in Cumberland in November, in a Manx boat, landing safely, Owen being their pilot. [Owen will have sailed up a large estuary, past Millom Castle, to Duddon Sands, outside Duddon Bridge near Broughton-in-Furness, where the River Duddon enters the sea.] He sold his goods upon the shore, and returned to Man in two and a half days. They had a violent storm in coming back, and every soul would have perished if it had not been for Owen's handling of the vessel. His next voyage was

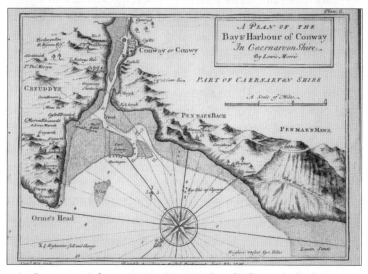

At Conwy on 4 February 1744, Owen purchased a fast yacht the Dispatch *and fitted it out for smuggling*

The Liverpool Arms on Conwy quayside, existed in Owen's time

for Barmouth in North Wales, with a large venture of tea, as well as a considerable sum of money that his wife had given him to buy a vessel. He landed safely, and went towards Westchester [– Chester's prominence in North-West England meant that many people called it thus], where he sold the last of his venture. Then Owen went down to Conwy in Caernarvonshire, in order to buy a gentleman's yacht there, the property of Squire Pugh of Plas Penrhyn. [This is confirmed in a later chapter] Owen bought her, the yacht [the *James and Bridget*] being a pretty thing, mounted several small guns, and arrived safely back at the Isle of Man.

His next expedition was to South Wales, with a full load of tun goods [large barrels of wine etc.] He provided himself with small arms and other necessaries for fighting, arriving safely in St. Bride's Bay at Coaltop Road anchorage, on the 12th March 1744. He sold the great part of his cargo, then came with the remainder to Cardigan Bay, and on his passage there was like to be cast away. When he came to Cardigan Bay, the king's cruiser was sent out to him, Owen, seeing her coming, clasped a spring upon his cable rope, and fired a shot at her. The cruiser took little notice, so Owen fired a broadside, which made them go back faster than they came. Owen went into the harbour that night and landed all his goods just next to the Custom House. He had carts and horses ready, sent them away with the goods and afterwards moored his vessel in the River Teifi.

The Collector of Cardigan, being a proud and haughty man, would not put up with this treatment of Owen's. He gathered together about twenty men, four of whom were Spaniards, prisoners-of-war in Cardigan Gaol, and two convicts from the gaol. The rest were one tide officer, supernumerary catch-poles, and informers, all well-armed. On the road coming to the vessel, they agreed to send a Spaniard to shoot Owen in his bed. They entered the vessel on the 4th of April 1744, with the dawning of the day. As soon as they entered, they began to cut down the rigging, threw the guns overboard, and stole everything they could find. Owen gave them all the fair words he was master of. A convict placed a pistol against his breast, and snapped it at him. As Owen held out a bottle of ale for them to drink, they ordered a Spaniard with a drawn cutlass (to cut his arm off), which he narrowly escaped. Owen begged for his life, but they swore they could kill him, but by this time the vessel had floated and sheared to the river. All his hands had run away and hid themselves except William Lewis. Owen asked if he would stand by him, and Lewis answered 'I will to the death!'

Then, the attack began. Owen fired up [from below decks] and they fired down, until Owen and Lewis had killed four and wounded several others. Then Owen and Lewis came upon deck. The rest had jumped overboard, leaving on deck thirty-five firearms, as well as fifteen cutlasses. There were four corpses, two Spanish and two Welsh, and one wounded convict [the deserter James Moss], who Owen took with him at the man's earnest request. Four days after that, the wind came fair, and Owen sailed for the Isle of Man, where he arrived safely. He put the convict in lodgings, got a surgeon to dress his wounds, gave him a suit of clothes, and paid for his diet and the surgeon. As soon as he was well, to requite Owen for his kindness, the convict went to the authorities and swore against him. Then there was an order issued out by the Governor of the island, to take Owen with his crew, and confine them [documented in a later chapter]. Owen being very well beloved among gentle and simple people, word was sent to him to get out of the way. He absconded, but they took two of his hands into custody. Owen was for some time shifting from place to place, the law of the island being so severe on such occasions. A man dare not, on penalty of death, give any assistance to a man under such accusation. But Owen, being well beloved among the population, was yet not informed upon.

His vessel had been seized in the king's name, along with all he had. The weather was very tempestuous, and as he could not get off the island there was a watch on all the seaports. Owen greatly reflected on himself, for not taking the counsel that was given him by his new wife, to leave off smuggling. He was at last, put to so hard shifts to live, none daring to harbour him, that he sheltered himself in the caves in the sea cliffs. His poor new wife would not part from him, but endured all these hardships with him. One day there was an order for every man on the island to search for him, every parish to meet at sun rising, and to be sworn to use their utmost endeavours to take him. His wife used to go in the night and provide meat for him. That day Owen went over a great cliff, and down to a cave where a man had never been before. His wife followed him as he went into the cave. The tide was out, then the tide coming in brought the spring tide, so the pair were in danger of drowning. He climbed up in the cave, hanging on by his two hands, and she hung to his waist, for upwards of an hour. The tide beginning to ebb, they came down to the water, and narrowly escaped drowning.

The weather grew more moderate, and an oyster boat belonging to the north of Ireland came by, and took them both in. They made for Strangford in the north of Ireland. The boat being small, and the seas high, several times they came close to sinking, but after eight hours passage arrived safely at Strangford Lough, and landed upon a man's island there. The next day they went to Downpatrick and took lodgings. They stayed there for a while, Owen pretending to be a yarn dealer, going by the name of Kennedy, a Scotsman. His landlord found by his language that he was no Scotsman, but a man well bred, and much of a gentleman. The neighbourhood conjectured that he had run away with an heiress and that they were incognito. He had not been there long, before some of the chief persons of the place came and conversed with him. They found him a man of sense, and who could talk well upon any subject, his conversation being quite agreeable. They took a great liking to him, and his wife, again, was so well respected by her own sex.

By this time Owen was advertised in all the public newspapers with a reward of a hundred pounds for the taking of him and expresses were sent to all the seaports in Ireland to take him. [The *London Gazette* of May 8-12 1744 reported the offer]. The Collector of Strangford had information against him, but Owen heard of it and went off privately, then resolved to go further inland. This was the latter end of May 1744. He put on a mean habit and went into Lurgan town in Armagh, his wife doing the same. On the road to Lurgan, he met a lad who sold scissors, pen-knives, spectacles, buckles, shirt buttons &co. Owen bought his box with all his goods for thirty shillings, and bartered with him for an old pair of leather breeches for a pair of cloth ones. When he came to Lisburn town, his wife bought a flannel gown, coarse linens, and other things necessary to make her look mean [poor]. She likewise bought a parcel of gartering laces, points, and a bundle of collars, resolving to take each of these trades for fear of discovery till affairs would cool a little, being afraid of going near any seaport, for fear of being known.

When they came to Lurgan, they went to a mean lodging, such as suited their profession, and Owen passed for a West of Ireland man by the name of Sulivan. He continued there for three months, following the markets and fairs constantly, carrying his box of goods in his ragged dress, his wife selling her long laces alongside him. At the end of three months, Owen resolved to go to Wales, in order to be properly advised what to do, and whether it would be safe or not to surrender and take his trial. He went by way of Dublin, where he was detained for some time by contrary winds. He took private lodgings in an outer part of the city, passing for an attorney from the north of Ireland, going to London to defend in a law suit. This passed very well. He left his wife there and landed safe in Wales. He went to his friends and discussed with them what to do. He was satisfied that it was safe for him to take his trial, so determined to advertise himself against the next Commission of Oyer and Terminer. [This was a commission issued to judges, to try cases on assize. It became obsolete with the abolition of assizes and the establishment of Crown Courts in 1972. It was also the name given to the court in which such a hearing was held.] But he absconded for the sake of his liberty, returning to Ireland in a small boat, enduring a great deal of hardship. He was received with all tenderness by his poor woman, and told the landlord he had won the lawsuit.

A few days after that, the landlord and a few creditable

dealers from the neighbourhood, took a coach and went to a fair six miles away, where Owen played the French horn and German flute [The German flute originated in Asia, spreading to Germany and France, being a transverse flute, rather than a recorder-type flute]. In all Owen was master of both music and dancing, performing a jig and a minuet, with his wife posing as a famous dancer. They both danced the jig and minuet, to the satisfaction of all the landlord's companions. Owen then resolved to go privately with a friend to the Isle of Man, about some other material business and arrived there safely. He continued undiscovered there for some time, but the weather being bad, he could not sail off, and was at last discovered and fled to the mountains. One day there came a company of soldiers to take him, finding out where Owen was, and approached him. Owen stripped [for action] and came pretty near them, putting his scimitar into the ground. He said 'My brave, manly men, why have so many of you come to destroy poor William Owen, who never offended or hurt you? Do you not remember the brave account of your forefathers, their valour, honour and courage? Even the women took to the field, and fought like lions. Have you none of their blood left in you? If you have, do not destroy me.' Consulting together, they all turned back and left him.

He continued in the hills (his wife had come over to join him), while his wife brought him relief. However she was taken and confined, for carrying meat to him. Owen continued in the hills for four days and nights without any subsistence, and in winter season. He was at last obliged to surrender, going to the governor, and was closely confined in Castle Rushen [in Castletown, the ancient capital of Man, it is one of the best preserved mediaeval castles in the world], but well treated. His poor new wife was always attending him, crying so much that she could hardly see. He was confined there for the space of two months. Then a king's messenger came for him and his three hands previously arrested, and brought them to Liverpool. Then they were removed to the city of Hereford and after a confinement of some months, he was tried at Hereford on 23rd March 1745, and a very severe prosecution was carried against him by the Commissioners of the Customs. Owen made a tolerable defence, having very much gained the affection of the country. On his trial the gentlemen spectators and indeed the judge himself were astonished to hear Owen plead for himself with such good language, and so much pertaining to the purpose, not expecting the like from a mariner. Owen was honourably acquitted after a trial of twelve hours, and the bells were rung with joy for his acquittal. His poor Manx wife had followed him to Hereford, bringing him a considerable sum of money. [He was actually convicted of manslaughter of the Cardigan Customs Officer, but seems to have been almost immediately released, perhaps with his wife paying a large fine].

He went from Hereford to the Isle of Man, where there was great rejoicing to see him, and took a house in the town of Douglas. Resolved to have another smuggling expedition, Owen sailed with a cargo of tun goods, along with three others to South Wales. He returned to Man in a short time with a cargo of corn, having made a successful voyage. Being persuaded by his wife to leave off that way of trading, he then sailed with his vessel as a packet between Man and Dublin, and continued that trade for the season, according to his agreement. Towards the latter end of September 1745 he resolved to sail with some tun goods for South Wales, not in his own vessel, but with one of his cousins [probably Ellis Owen]. He had a law suit pending between himself and another person, and was obliged to leave his wife's sister's son to go on a venture with his cousins. [Owen states that 'he was obliged to leave his wife's sister son'. Did he mean that he was obliged to leave his 'wife' with her sister-in-law who lived at Liverpool whom she had visited before?] They sailed out of the island on 2nd October, and on the 3rd in the morning there arose a violent storm, and in the dead of that night the vessel was cast away. Every soul perished – how, nobody could tell. The mast was found broken, above the deck, a piece of the boat was found and some of its goods were floating and taken, which was liquor. The country people made merry on it, but not one of the bodies was ever found.

Owen continued in the island for some time expecting his wife's return, remaining there until the latter end of November. Having no news, he resolved to find out what had happened to them, sailing to Liverpool and then making for South Wales. He could get no intelligence of them until he came between Aberdovey [Aberdyfi] and Llanbadarn [near Aberystwyth]. He met a seafaring man he knew, and asked him if he knew anything of such a vessel. The mariner told him that they had been cast away nearly two months ago, and every soul of them perished [possibly sailing to Liverpool from Man]. This he confirmed to be true. Owen then grieved from his heart, so great was his love for that woman. Since he had first lived with her, he had left off seeing lewd women. Apart from the loss of his wife, he lost upwards of £160. When Owen came to Pembrokeshire he found everything the sailor had told him to be true, and his grief was so great that he could not eat, drink or sleep for some time. He remained in the country among his friends until March, and then sailed for Dublin. Here he fell in with a gentleman's kept mistress, and conveyed her to his lodgings. The gentleman came, having received intelligence of where she was, and with whom, and resolved to murder Owen, who narrowly escaped.

Owen then shipped as master of a vessel, making two voyages in that station, then left her. He next was master of a twenty gun Liverpool privateer, the *Admiral Blake*. In July 1746, they sailed on their respective cruise from Cork. In the January following, they came into Cobh, the port in County Cork, having had very little success. [Owen calls this Cove. The port was first called 'Cove', or the 'The Cove of Cork' in 1750, but renamed Queenstown in 1849 to commemorate a visit by Queen Victoria. In 1920, it was renamed Cobh by the Irish Free State, Cobh being a Gaelic version of the English name Cove.] The crew had met with great sickness, attended by vast mortality, off the Barbary Coast. Owen was very ill when they sailed into Cobh, and retired sick to his quarters. When he had recovered a little, he made for Dublin, but on the road there got a fresh cold, which led to a relapse. He continued, very ill, in Dublin for some time. Everything he had was sold and pledged [pawned]. His friends took little notice of him when his money was gone. He then stayed in a widow woman's house, who gave him a little credit, otherwise he would have starved. When he left, he made for Liverpool, where he stayed for some time. His doctors told him that he would not be fit for service at sea to act as master, until towards June.

Then Owen resolved to see his friends and acquaintances in Wales, with the design to stay there until he recovered his health. When he came to South Wales, he met upon the road one James Lilly, a fencing master, and they travelled together for a while. There were some other persons upon the road, about a hundred yards away from them. [This was the men forming a *hue and cry*, noted in Chapter 4]. Lilly was on horseback, and Owen on foot, when these men heard a shot, and saw Lilly fall off with a pistol in his hand. Owen also had a pistol in his hand. The wound was mortal, and Lilly died a few hours later. Owen was taken, examined, sent to gaol, and tried in Carmarthen on Friday the 17th of April 1747. He was found guilty of murder and received sentence of death for the same. Owen denied the fact, but was found guilty by a great many circumstances. A great many believed him innocent. He was then thirty years of age.

The Character and Behaviour of Captain William Owen

William Owen was a man of five foot and a half high, well made, clean limbed, with a pretty long visage, fair complexion, a very proud spirited man, very humble in his behaviour; very hospitable and very revengeful for the time, but of a forgiving temper; a little passionate formerly, but of late years otherwise, entirely by reasoning with himself, he overcomes passion. When he was angry he would look very fierce, but whenever he would be going to an engagement, he would be very cool with a smiling countenance, never tasting anything that is strong at such times, and never was known drunk. He was seemingly a bashful man and never would make free with any man before he did know him well; never given to swearing nor quarrelling, but very much to whoring, which proved his ruin. He had a notion when he was going on any enterprise, that the enemy could not kill him; he had his share of natural sense, pretty good learning very agreeable in his conversation, very sincere to his friend, more generosity than ability. At the same time, he had a great deal of inward feeling, but soon forgot himself. He never would be advised by his father, yet thought every man wiser than himself till he had proved them. In his latter days he proved a great penitent, reflected greatly on his youthful transactions. He was greatly respected by all men of valour, and as much disrespected by all cowards; he had a great many friends, and so many adversaries, especially the officers of both custom house and excise.

He was very loyal in the main, for he refused a major's commission in the rebel army in the year 1745*. His carriage was very grand, it was very remarkable when he was but eight years of age his mind was entirely bent upon military exercises, and was always (when from school) exercising himself, he was thought by most people that knew him or have had conversation with him, to have been a very good natured man, in the last year and half of his days he was very serious and thoughtful, so that a man would think him (at some particular times) to be quite melancholy; some people thought it was the death of his wife that he had taken to heart, others would say it was his loss and the aspersion of his adversaries. [*Bonnie Prince Charles landed in Scotland 23 July 1745, and took Edinburgh on 17 September. On 8 November, his army entered England and took Carlisle on 22 December. The bloody Battle of Culloden on 16 April 1746 ended all hope of another Stuart king. This claim by Owen seems to be braggadocio, as he does not mention it in the events of 1745, when his fortunes were at a low ebb all year].

Owen's exploits were acted as a play on several stages, at such towns as Whitehaven, Workington, Carlisle, Kendal, Lancaster, Dublin & in relation to his engagement with the Whitehaven cruiser & co, which actors got a great deal of money, by the same. [This last sentence may well have been added after Owen's death, and copies of the play have not as yet been found].

[The above was written in a period of around two weeks, from his conviction of 16 April until his hanging on 2 May, as noted above. There follows in Owen's manuscript confession the following transcript. The trial seems to have had a foregone conclusion, despite Owen's spirited and coherent defence, and he could well have been acquitted today. It seems that the authorities knew of his other crimes, and the verdict was to save further charges being processed. Thus the charges of killing the Cardigan Post-Boy Evan George and badly injuring/killing the Nevern manservant were never pursued.]

William Owen, eighteenth-century Welsh smuggler (National Library of Wales MS 21834B) – Transcript of the account of the trial of William Owen at Carmarthen Great Sessions, April 1747 Proceedings on the King's Commission of the Peace, Oyer and Terminer and Goal Delivery held at Carmarthen

Vincent's account of Owen's last words

William Owen was taken prisoner the sixth day of April 1747 in the county of Carmarthen near Lampeter, and committed to Carmarthen Castle on suspicion of killing the Cardigan Post, but not charged then with the killing of Lilly, he was then very sickly and had but three shillings in the world, and would not send to his friends for relief, for what reason we cannot tell: One Daniel James there being gaoler, a very hospitable man, took compassion upon him, and found him with necessaries. [In 1756 Daniel James was bound over to appear before court for helping two prisoners escape]. Two days before the Assizes the return of the coroner's inquest was sent to the gaoler, which had brought Owen in guilty of the murder of Lilly, which inquest the gaoler shewed to Owen.

On Wednesday the 16th of the said month in the morning the bill was found by the grand jury against Owen. In the evening he was brought to the bar, to be arraigned. The Court being set, the prisoner being brought to court.

Clerk of the Crown Cryer, make proclamation, command every person to keep silent on pain of imprisonment.

Clerk of the Court. Jailor, bring Wm Owen to the bar (the prisoner being brought). Wm Owen hold up thy hand, you stand there indicted by the name of Wm Owen late of St Dogmael in the county of Pembroke, mariner.

Prisoner. With humble submission my Lords, I humbly beg that your Lordships may have the patience to hear, what I the poor prisoner at the bar has to say?

Judges. We will hear you, go on prisoner.

Prisoner. With humble submission my Lords, I stand here indicted for the murder of James Lilly. I was not committed, my Lords, on suspicion of that fact that I stand indicted for; neither did I know that any such prosecution was to be carried on against me till Friday last. [He was originally indicted for the killing of Evan George in the hue and cry]. I have not had time sufficient to summons my witnesses to appear here, by reason of the great distance they are off. Some, my Lords, are in Pembrokeshire and some in Cardiganshire. I am innocent of the fact, but how my Lords is it possible for me to make my innocence appear to your Lordships, and my country? Except your Lordships' great goodness and benevolence will take this my present poor helpless case into consideration, and postpone my trial till the next assizes: I have neither my Lords, counsellors nor solicitors to plead for me.

Judges. If you want counsel prisoner, there is counsel in court, choose your counsel.

Prisoner. I have no money my Lords to retain counsel.

Judges. Have you any one in court to make affidavit that you had not time sufficient to get your witnesses, and that you could not get them here by this day?

Prisoner. Only my own affidavit my Lords.

King's Counsel. My lords, I am concerned for the King against the prisoner at the bar. The law sayeth, it must be made appear by the affidavit of another person, and not by the affidavit of the prisoner.

Prisoner. With humble submission my Lords I am no lawyer, neither do I understand the law, but my vulgar reason makes me believe that our happy constitution is grounded upon good men's consciences and consciences upon reason, reason on equity; I presume to say my Lords, that in equity I should have time to have got my witnesses.

Judges. Prisoner, we can give no longer time because you have no affidavit – Jailer take care of the prisoner, and bring him to the bar at nine o'clock in the morning with his irons off.

On the 17th at nine o'clock in the morning, the court set, the prisoner was brought to court.

Clerk of the Crown. Jailer bring Wm Owen to the bar – Wm Owen hold up thy hand. You stand there indicted by the name of Wm Owen late of St Dogmael in the county of Pembroke, mariner. Having not the fear of God before your eyes, you did wilfully discharge a loaded pistol with a leaden ball valued at five shillings, at James Lilly late of the town of Cardigan, which ball entered the body of the said James Lilly, in the pit of the stomach, and made a hole therein of half an inch wide, and seven inches deep, in the parish of Llanhenell [this is Lanfihangel-ar-Arth, pronounced in the past by locals as Llaningell] in the county of Carmarthen on the sixth day of this month, of which wound he the said Lilly expired, in a short time after. – What sayest thou, are you Guilty of this fact, or not Guilty?

Prisoner. Not Guilty.

Clerk of the Crown. Who will you be tried by?

Prisoner. God and my country.

Clerk of the Crown. God send you a safe deliverance.

Clerk of the Crown. Call the list of the jurymen over.

Judges. Prisoner if you have any objections to make against any of the jury, you may choose twelve of thirty-six.

Prisoner. I am my Lords an entire stranger in this county. I am satisfied as they are called.

Clerk of the Crown. Jurors look at the prisoner, – Prisoner look upon the jurors, – the jury being sworn.

King's Council. My Lords we will call our witness, and prove the fact that the prisoner stands indicted for. – call John Franklin.

Witness [John Franklin]. John Franklin deposes that he on the sixth of that month, about the hour of six o'clock in the morning, saw the prisoner at the bar and James Lilly coming through Llangeler in the said county. [Llangeler is in Carmarthenshire, between Dre-fach Velindre and Llandysul]. Lilly was on horseback, and the prisoner on foot, with a leather cap on and about his face. He farther deposes that about the hour of nine o'clock the same morning there came several people by, some on foot and some on horseback, and asked if we saw the murderers. The witness asked who, and they said they were William Owen and James Lilly. Witness said that they went by about six o'clock in the morning. Witness deposes, that he and another joined and went in pursuit of them, and about the hour of twelve saw them on the hills. When they came within about a hundred yards off them, the witness deposes, that Lilly was on horseback, and Owen the prisoner on foot. They stopped, talking to one another, face to face, and pretty close to each other. The witness said he heard a shot, which he took to be out of a pistol, and saw Lilly drop off the horse, on the same side as the prisoner stood, and saw the prisoner turn round with something in his hand, that shined, which he took to be a pistol. The horse made off, the prisoner pursued the horse, and mounted him. The witness further said, that he came pretty near Lilly, who was lying on the ground with a pistol in his hand.

David Oliver being called, who deposed to the same purpose as John Franklin, only the distance which he proved about two or three yards the prisoner stood from Lilly, when the pistol was discharged. Neither could not say whether by Lilly or the prisoner it was discharged.

Judges. Prisoner, have you any questions to ask John Franklin?

Prisoner. Yes, my lords, with humble submission to your lordships, I have several questions to ask. If your Lordships please, to ask John Franklin if he had any personal knowledge of me before that day that Lilly was killed.

Witness [David Oliver]. No not before that day.

Prisoner. I humbly beg that your lordships, may be pleased to ask him, if he knows my face?

Judges. John Franklin look at the prisoner, do you know his face?

Witness. No I do not.

Prisoner. What knowledge have you of me?

Witness. Cap, person and coat.

Prisoner. I humbly beg that your lordships may be pleased to ask, what distance he was off when the supposed pistol was then discharged?

Witness. About four score or a hundred yards.

Prisoner. What part of the horse was towards him then?

Witness. I was rather before the horse, on the left hand side, with all.

Prisoner. How near was I, when the supposed pistol was fired; at the deceased James Lilly?

Witness. I cannot tell exactly – you were pretty close.

Prisoner. Does he take upon him to say that I fired it?

Witness. I do not know how it was fired, but a shot went off.

Prisoner. On what side of the horse was I when the pistol was fired?

Witness. The right side of the horse.

The next witness for the crown that was called was Thomas Phillips, who deposes that he came thereabouts six o'clock, and saw James Lilly lying on the ground, then alive, but in great agony, and several others with him. And that the said Lilly had a wound in the right side of his temples, which he thought he had received by a pistol ball, and that he had another in the pit of his stomach, out of which wound there came blood as he breathed, which he thought was the mortal wound.

Judges. Prisoner, have you any questions to ask the witness?

Prisoner. Yes my Lords, with humble submission, I have great many questions to ask him. If your Lordships please to ask him, if the wound in the head had bruised the skull or not?

Witness [Thomas Phillips]. No the skull was not hurt, it went slantways, upwards.

Prisoner. Please to ask him, my lords, whether the wound in the stomach went slanting upwards, or downwards, or sideways or right in the body.

Witness. The wound went directly in, neither one way, nor the other but direct, and through his coat and waistcoat.

Prisoner. Were his coat and waistcoat burnt by powder, when the wound was given, as you can judge?

Witness. Yes, both his coat and waistcoat were burnt.

Prisoner. Had he a pistol by him when you saw him?

Witness. No not one as I saw.

The next witness for the Crown, was one John Thomas, who deposes that the prisoner and the deceased Lilly, came by his house about ten o'clock, and desired to have some victuals. He gave them victuals, and directed them in the road. In the evening it was reported abroad, that a man was killed upon the hills, and that he went to the place where he lay, and found Lilly with a great many people about him, and he was alive. He declared much to the same purpose as the other witness.

Judges. Prisoner have you any questions to ask this witness?

Prisoner. Yes, my Lords with submission I have several questions to ask him. If your Lordships please to ask him, if I seemed to have any anger at Lilly when in his house?

Witness [John Thomas]. No, not the least that I could see or hear, but seemed they very loving with one another.

Prisoner. How was the wound in his head, do you think he had that wound on him in your house?

Witness. No, he had not.

Prisoner. How was the wound in the breast, and was his coat and waistcoat burnt?

Witness. His coat and waistcoat was burnt, and the wound was directly in.

Judges. Gentlemen for the Crown, have you any more witnesses to call?

Counsel for the Crown. No my Lords we have no more.

Judges. Prisoner, have you any witnesses to call in your defence.

Prisoner. Yes, my Lords, John Davies of Blanerdon.

Judges. What question will you have us to ask him?

Prisoner. If your lordships please to ask him; whether he was summoned there or no, to view the corpse, and if he was sworn to the same.

Witness [John Davies]. Yes, I and another freeholder, were charged there and sworn to view the corpse.

Prisoner. How was the wound in the pit of the stomach, directly in, or slantways?

Witness. Direct in the body.

Prisoner. How was his coat, was it burnt, or scorched?

Witness. A large piece, quite through the coat, was burnt.

Prisoner. Is it to be supposed or thought, that a man at two yards distance, could give him that wound?

Witness. No, I think not for I think that the pistol must have been close to his coat.

Judges. Prisoner have you any further questions to ask?

Prisoner. No my Lords nothing else

Judges. Have you any more evidence to produce?

Prisoner. No, my Lords, there is no-one in town as I know of.

Judges. Council for the King, have you any observations to make?

Council for the Crown. Nothing more, my Lords.

Judges. Prisoner have you any observations to make?

Prisoner. Yes with your Lordships leave, the first evidence for the Crown, my Lords which was John Franklin, deposed that he was before the horse; with all said, and that I was close to the deceased Lilly. With humble submission my Lords, I take upon me to say that a man at such a distance, bearing upon a line with two men, may judge these two to be six or eight yards nearer then they would. Neither, my Lords, did he say that I killed him, or discharged the supposed pistol.

Judges. Prisoner, have you any more to say? Speak up.

Prisoner. It's plainly made to appear, my Lords, by the evidence of John Thomas that the deceased James Lilly and I had no spite or malice one or the other. It appeared my Lords, by the cross examination of John Franklin that I was on the right side of the horse. And all the witnesses agreed, who viewed the corpse, that the wound went into the body direct, as appeared likewise by his clothes. My Lords, they likewise all agreed that the coat and waistcoat was burnt, in particular, it appeared so by the evidence of Mr John Davies, who was sworn to view the corpse that the coat was burnt through.

Judges. Prisoner, proceed if you have anything more to say.

Prisoner. With humble submission my Lords, as I was on the right side of the horse, it was impossible for me to give him that wound, in the pit of the stomach Be pleased to hear me, as I was on the right side, I could not discharge a piece that would penetrate direct into the body, it must have gone slantways to the left side and upwards. My Lords with humble submission, I shall give your Lordships further reason for it. My Lords, as he was on horseback and I on foot, and he upon a large horse, and he being a great deal taller than I, I must be my Lords too low by a great deal to discharge a piece that would directly go into the body. It must have gone upwards, for when a man discharges a piece, he cannot lift that piece higher than his eye. If he does, my Lords, he will be aimless. In relation to the burning of the coat, I take upon me to say, for I have proved it by experience that if the muzzle of a piece be but half a foot off the body it will not burn through cloth. And as it appeared by the evidence of David Oliver, that he judged me to be two or three yards off Lilly, when the supposed pistol was discharged. So I trust in your Lordships great consideration, that all the facts when compared, can never bring me in Guilty of his death.

Judges. Prisoner, have you any further observations to make?

Prisoner. I humbly beg to be heard in one thing more, my Lords.

Judges. We will hear you, for you have a right to speak, being as you have no counsel.

Prisoner. With humble submission, my Lords, I humbly presume to say upon this melancholy juncture of mine, that my adversaries embraced this opportunity, in throwing all the ill-natured aspersions as they are capable of saying of me to my injury. Permit my Lords to say that I am a mariner bred, and have had the pleasure of serving in His Majesty's Royal Navy some years: and likewise my Lords have served in the Merchants' employment for a considerable time, and have been in many enterprises, especially in America, and by all those that employed me I was always respected. I was likewise, my Lords, master of a vessel for many years, employed by several merchants of different parts; my last expedition was in the *Blake* Privateer of Liverpool. In July last I went out as master of her, and came home in January last as first lieutenant of her. Now my Lords I stand here indicted for that heinous crime of murder, which crime I am innocent of. I presume my Lords to say, that I put all my adversaries to their defiance, to make it appear that ever I committed or attempted a barbarous act, but always discharged my trust, with honour.

Council for the Crown. My Lords we do not in behalf of the Crown prosecute the prisoner for his character, but for the murder of James Lilly.

Judges. Prisoner have you anything else to observe?

Prisoner. No my Lords, I have nothing else.

Judges. Jury hear to the charge against the prisoner at the bar, and the evidence that was given for and against him.

The judges, having read the deposition of the witnesses to the jury, told them to consider whether the prisoner was guilty or not. The jury withdrew, and after some debate among them, brought the prisoner a verdict of guilty of murder.

Judges. Take care of prisoner jailor, and bring him to court at four o'clock in the afternoon.

The court being set, the prisoner being brought to court.

Judges. William Owen what cause have you to shew, why sentence of death should not be pronounced against you?

Prisoner. I have, my Lords, several causes to show. I had not time to get my witness, which witness would have proved that they saw Lilly giving himself the mortal wound by discharging a pistol at himself, and I believe that there are several points of law that I hope will arise in my favour.

Judges. As to your witnesses you had time to bring them. But to the aforesaid points of law, what are they?

Prisoner. My Lords I am no lawyer, neither do I understand the law, for that reason I cannot plead the law.

Judges. Have you any farther cause to show?

Prisoner. No my Lords, I have nothing farther.

Judges. William Owen, you were indicted for the murder of James Lilly, you threw yourself upon your country, which country found you Guilty. You are to go from thence to whence you came from thence to the place of execution, and there be hanged by the neck, Dead, Dead, Dead: 'The Lord have mercy on your soul.'

Prisoner. My Lords, I have the greatest concern to me, to pray for of your Lordships. Your Lordships has performed your duties, in pronouncing sentence of death on me. Permit me, worthy Lords, to say that I have spent my youthful days quite negligent of my duty towards my great Creator; in pity to my poor immortal spirit: I pray for the sake of Jesus Christ for a fortnight's extraordinary [extra time before hanging], in order to enable me to make my peace with my great Creator, who I the unworthy creature hath so often offended.

Judges. That will be considered upon, Jailor take care of the prisoner.

On the 28th the jailor came by their Lordships' commands to the prisoner; and told him, that he was commanded by the judges to tell him that the day of his execution was appointed to be on Saturday the second day of May. The prisoner made answer, if the day for the execution of my body is fixed so soon,

I thank God the day of execution on my soul is not at their Lordships' commands.'

It seems very much that Owen's spirited and reasoned defence could have caused reasonable doubt in the judges' minds, but that they had already decided that another trial, concerning the murder of Evan George, the leading chaser in the hue and cry, was not worth their trouble. Owen had caused enough mayhem across the land, and they had come to their verdict before the trial.

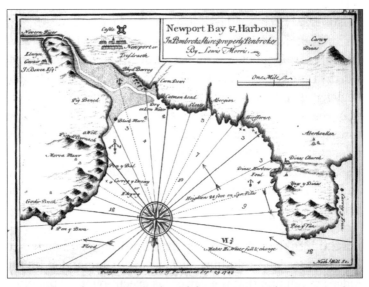

Owen knew this coast intimately, and the Rev. Vincent of Newport Castle wrote an account of his life

Chapter 3

The Account of Owen's Life by the Rev. Henry J. Vincent

This is taken from an unpublished manuscript *A History of St Dogmael's* (NLW 5603B), by the Reverend Henry J. Vincent of Newport Castle. It was compiled around 1860. Glen Johnson has recorded Vincent's career in detail, which begins: 'On 1st August 1826 Rev. Henry James Vincent became the Vicar of St. Dogmaels, Monington and Llantood until 1865. On Whitsunday 1827 the new Vicar ended the practice of ball games taking place in the churchyard annually on that feast day, by positioning two constables at each entrance to the site...' (*glen-johnson. co.uk/parish-church-of-st-thomas/*). We should be indebted to Vincent, as about 1850 he found in the wall of his vicarage the white-washed *Sagrani Maqi Cunatam* pillar-stone, which had been previously used as a gate-post and bridge. While removing the stone it fell and broke into two parts, hence its metal band. It is bilingual, in Latin and Ogham, and its discovery helped us translate the Ogham language used in Ireland and Briton between the 4th and 7th centuries CE. The language is phonetic and uses line patterns to represent each letter instead of characters that we use now. It is (the stone) of Sagragnus son of Cunatamus, with Sagranus having a link with St Saeran of Llanynys near Cilmeri in the Vale of Clwyd. (This is where Llywelyn ap Gruffudd celebrated Mass on the day of his murder in 1282).

Westwood in 1879 wrote: 'This stone has acquired a celebrity from having been the first discovered in Wales on which the debased Latin inscription was repeated in Celtic in Ogham characters, and having thence been considered by

Professor Graves, the first authority on the subject, to be as valuable a key to the latter mode of writing as the Rosetta stone was to Egyptian hieroglyphics'. The following account has probably been taken from local folklore, gathered from 1826 onwards, around eight decades after Owen's death, and only some punctuation has been added. This author's additions are in square brackets.

'A little above the village, [St Dogmael's] to the right of the road leading to Moylegrove is Ty hîr [this should be spelt Tŷ hir] long house, so called probably from the extreme length of the old House, which was replaced some years ago by the present building. This place is noted for having been the birthplace of William [Bowen is crossed out] Owen, commonly called Will Tyhîr, a notorious freebooter who infested this District about 150 years ago – a Book containing his history, or as some say his autobiography, was printed – some of the old people remember having seen it, and if it could now be found might prove an *Eldorado* [treasure trove] to novelists and poets, particularly to those who delight to expatiate [write in detail] on the exploits of Robbers of the Sea and land from Robin Hood and his Merry men to Jonathan Wild the corsair, Dick Turpin, Jack Sheppard and other worthies of the *Newgate Calendar*. [This was subtitled *The Malefactors' Bloody Register*, originally a monthly account of executions, but later expanded into biographical 'chapbooks' (small, popular, cheap books) of notorious criminals].

Our hero was a kind of amphibious animal exercising his dexterity ashore and afloat. It is said he commenced his career by pilfering gardens and other acts of petty larceny, and in performing practical jokes after the fashion of his countryman Twm Siôn Cathi [Cati]. He was Master of a small Vessel in the country trade, and he was on one occasion lying in Ramsey Sound waiting the tide. [Ramsey Sound is at the western end of St David's Peninsula between Ramsey Island and the mainland, a dynamic stretch of water with strong tidal currents and hazardous rocks]. He observed reapers on land overworked at the harvest and determined to give them a short Holiday – with this view he set up on Deck an image of straw draped in Sailor's clothes, and commenced belabouring it with a stick. When the reapers saw what was going on in the ship, although they were not sufficiently near to discover the trick, they immediately left their horses and ran down to the verge of the rock, crying Murder – Will having finished with the bastinado [beating with a stick, often practised on the soles of the feet as torture], took a pistol and shot overboard the image, to which a line was fastened (for the purpose of drawing it back), to the great horror of the reapers, who scarcely did anything for some hours, but watched the vessel and the appearance of the body.

The first serious act in the Drama of Will's eventful life was the murder at Bryndu [– the River Teifi used to be straight at Cardigan, between Bryndu and Pwll Cam]. The vessel of which he probably was Master was taken with contraband goods and brought to Bryndu; and put under the custody of a Customs House Officer of the name of Phillips and three Spanish prisoners from Cardigan Gaol. Will not approving of the Capture thus addressed the officer – 'Go ashore, Sir. I'll take you in the boat if you wish it – if not, I will shoot guns', and on the Officer refusing to relinquish his Duty, Will shot him dead. He also shot one of the Spaniards, wounded a boy, and calling his apprentice to brake loose [cut the ropes securing the ship], set to skull [row] the boat and come about [turn] and sail for some distant port. Some say he was taken, tried and acquitted which is scarcely probable, others that he escaped and was not heard of for a long time, until he subsequently wrote to his parents at Tyhir stating that he had been pressed on board a Man of War and enclosing a letter informing him that he had come to the possession of a large estate, and begging him to make haste home. His parents acceded to his wishes and when he received his letter, he lost no time in shewing it to the Captain, who congratulated him on his good fortune, and immediately set him free.

After his return home he commenced a regular system of free booting, in conjunction with a man of the name of Lily, the father of Miss Dolly who kept a boarding School at Cardigan about the beginning of the century. [This must be Dorothea Laugharne – see footnote on John Lilly]. This Lily lived at Tir Ffynnon and was married to Miss Askew, daughter of Mr Askew of Llanreithan near St David's. [The church of Rheithan, or Rhidian, and parish are four miles north-northeast of Solva]. When asked by Cecilia Galando [or Galendo, Galindo] of Swansea, the mother of Molly Martin the village postmistress, 'How can you marry such a vile man', [Miss Askew, now Mrs Lily] answered 'Look at his beautiful hands'. Though these hands were not soiled by money or labour, they had a moral filth which no water could wash away. Will and Lily '*arcade ambi*' [both rascally friends] were the terror of the country. On one occasion they robbed the post – they were said to be kind to the poor and helped them out of the rich man's coffers by taking the law entirely in their own hands.

At Pwllcastele there is a stone called carreg y lleidr – the thief's stone, where they were said to lie perdu [concealed], when they had occasion to escape the officers of justice. [Pwllcastell must be Castle Pool. The first of Cardigan's castles was believed to have been built as a Norman motte and bailey settlement around 1093 at the far end of the Teifi estuary, known as Castle Pool.]

During their absence from home, which was frequently the case, Mr Askew came to Tyrffynnon [sic] and asked his daughter for Lily. On being told he was not at home, he enquired where he kept his money – 'In yonder room' was the reply, 'but the door is locked.' 'I must have that opened', said Askew. A locksmith from the abbey [St Dogmael's] was sent for to open the door, and in a draw was found a large bag full of money, which Askew swore was stolen from him at Llanreithan, as he was able to identify the bag. A hue and cry commenced against the thieves, who were discovered in Carmarthen, and closely pursued by the officers of justice. They had but one horse between them, and Will who was on foot called on Lily to dismount, or he would shoot him.

But as Lily was flying for his life, he gave no heed to him, whereupon Will took out his pistol and, not having a ball, cut off one of the buttons of his coat. He put it in his pistol and shot Lily dead, mounted the horse and fled. The popular belief was that Lily had killed himself, he having frequently declared that the officers should not take him alive – but from the direction of the ball, and the fact that Will having been taken on Lily's horse, he was tried at Carmarthen and executed there. He was said to be the handsomest man ever seen, that his elocution was much above his station, that he displayed such skill in defending himself on his trial, that the judge expressed his deep regret that such eminent talents should have been so wretchedly abused. On the scaffold it is said that he gave out a Welsh Psalm.

> Trugaredd, f'Arglwydd, heb ddim mwy,
> Yw'r cwbl yr wy'n ei geisio;
> Trugaredd yw fy newis lwydd,
> Trugaredd, f'Arglwydd, dyro!

['Mercy, my Lord, with nothing more, / Is all I am seeking; / Mercy is my successful choice, / Mercy, my Lord, give!' This is the fifth and final verse of *Na thro dy ŵyneb Arglwydd glân* – O Lord turn not thy face away, by Rowland Fychan (1590-1667) translated in 2015 by Richard P. Gillion.]

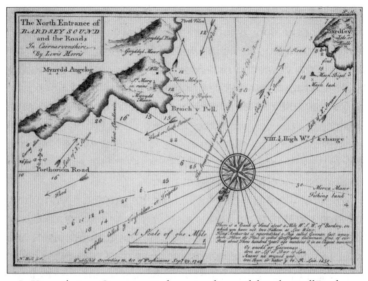

In Vincent's story, Owen regretted running down a fishing boat off Bardsey Island

It is said he appeared to be penitent, and that his greatest grief was his having sunk two vessels in the Bristol Channel, this affirms that what gave him the greatest sorrow was his having overrun a fishing boat near Bardsey Island, mistaking it for the coastguard, when all the crew perished. He was married to one of the Lloyds of Trevigin [Trefigin is in the hundred of Nevern, near St Dogmael's. It was in the eighteenth century home of the Lloyds of Trefigin, an offshoot of the Lloyds of Hendre, but only Trefigin Manor Farm survives. A *cwrt*, and Castell Trefigin are marked near Rhyd-Galed on a 1900 map]. The accounts respecting this man vary so much, that it would be very desirable that the book referred to should be found.'

Vincent's account is based upon stories from his parishioners more than a century after Owen's execution, and makes him out to be far less of a 'hero' than the 'confession'. It is interesting to note that Owen was pressed into service rather than being so brave in fighting an English man-of-war that his captain made him a midshipman. Vincent confuses James Lilly's marriage – it was to Anne Laugharne, not Askew, of Llanreithan. Owen married Ann Nicholas, not a Lloyd, unless there was bigamy involved here as well as with Mary Kelly. The tale of the robbery at Llanreithan may well be confused with Dorothea Laugharne taking some silver from the mansion, see the following note on James Lilly. I cannot as yet find any details of Cecilia Galando or Molly Martin, and there was no mention in the trial of Lilly being killed by a coat button. The Lilly family appears to be new to the Pembrokeshire area. There are many fragmented ends to the story of James Lilly and William Owen, which will take months to research, and need to be tied up by a better genealogist than this author.

A Note upon James Lilly

Often research leads one off on a tangent, and sometimes, as in the case of Lilly, it proves fruitful. Lilly had business dealings with Owen, which led to a court case against him, then ended up joining Owen in nefarious activities before he was shot by Owen. Many sources repeat that James Lilly had a brother John, also operating in south-west Wales at this time, but it strongly appears that no such brother existed. A search of records reveals no John and James Lilly siblings in England, Scotland and Wales at the time.

Our James Lilly, the only child of John Lilly, was baptised 3 September 1695 at Bromsgrove, Worcestershire. (There is one other potential James Lilly, born in Bishopsgate, London around 1700, whose father was Edward, but geography favours the Bromsgrove Lilly unless Lilly moved from London). He married Priscilla, the only child of William Earl(e) and Mary Null. (Her parents were married at St James, Dukes Place,

London on 21 July 1684.) Priscilla was baptised at Bromyard, Hereford on 24 April 1700, about 30 miles from Bromsgrove. Upon 6 February 1726 James Lilly and Priscilla Earl married at Hereford Cathedral, which indicates that it may have been a middle-class marriage. At some time Priscilla died, Lilly moved to south-west Wales and upon 30 November, 1735, Lilly married Anne Laugharne at Llanreithan.

Major Francis Jones wrote of James Lilly marrying a daughter from the Llanreithan estate, which led to the discovery that Lilly had no brother. Llanreithan had been a seat of the Bowens at the time of Henry VII, but by the 18th century was in Laugharne hands. Walter Laugharne died in 1726, leaving the mansion to his wife Elizabeth and a substantial estate to his eldest son John Laugharne. The second son William entered the church, and there was a dowry granted to Walter's three daughters, Anne, Dorothy and Margaret. John, High Sheriff of Pembroke in 1731, was to be the last squire of Llanreithan, being involved with court cases against his mother and sisters. Jones writes that John Laugharne was anxious to preserve the estate but circumstances meant that he had financial problems – 'Although he maintained his brother and sisters, he found it difficult to supply them with ready money and this resulted in disputes and misunderstandings. In these clashes, the mother [Elizabeth Laugharne] took the part of the younger children.'

Jones wrote of James Lilly of Haverfordwest, 'a dancing master and, occasionally, a teacher of drawing. His activities brought him into contact with the gentry to whose children he taught these accomplishments, and in due course met Miss Anne Laugharne of Llanreithan. They took a fancy to each other, and despite her brother's strongly expressed objections, Anne married her swain at Llanreithan church on 30 November 1735. [He would have been around forty years old]. From Lilly's point of view, it was an advantageous union, particularly as he could now rely on his wife's dowry to satisfy certain creditors who had sued him for debt a month or two before the marriage. John Laugharne, and his kinsfolk at Llanunwas, Pontfaen and St Brides were scandalised by the mésalliance, and some half a century later William Laugharne of Llanunwas, in his will, told his heirs – "I positively enjoin them that they never leave a single half penny, nor foot of, what I leave them, to the spurious blood of the supposed Lillys sprung from the loins of the late Mrs Anne Laugharne of Llanreithan."' [In the Eaton Evans papers, George Roch of Butterhill, St Ishmaels (*D-EE/40/138/B*) has the will of William Laugharne, the Rector of Dinas. 'Laugharne made bequests to three female servants, and left properties and bequests to his sisters Elizbeth, Margarett and Corbetta Laugharne. He requested to be buried in the same grave as "my dear wife" at Whitchurch in Dewisland Church. Of particular interest is his anger almost thirty years after James Lilly's death. He specified that nothing should be given to the Williams family of Trecadwgan or to the 'spurious blood of the supposed Lillys...']

Jones writes: 'After marriage the Lillys settled at Haverfordwest, later moved to Cardigan Town... James Lilly was a burgess of the town. (Footnoted is 'They had seven children – William, baptized 9 September 1735 [baptised at St Mary's, Haverfordwest, who emigrated to Newfoundland, or possibly North Carolina in 1763]; Abel; Essex; Elizabeth [who married John Richards of Cardigan 8 January 1764 and] died on 5 October 1767, aged 29; Margaret alive in 1764; Dorothy who died on 16 June 1801 aged 56 [so born c.1745]; and Anne who was alive in 1764 [married at Ludchurch, Pembrokeshire on 13 August 1756, lived at Lampeter] – M.I.'). In Haverfordwest they were joined by Mrs [the widowed] Elizabeth Laugharne and her other two daughters [Dorothy and Margaret]. In due course these daughters followed their sister's dubious example by marrying below themselves. Margaret, at the age of 29, married in 1743 Daniel Benbow, a needy attorney at law from Aberystwyth, who afterwards settled in Haverfordwest [widowed in 1764, died without issue]; and on 8 October 1749, Dorothy was married at St Thomas's Church, Haverfordwest, to John Ashwell of Lincolnshire, described by her furious brother as "a tramp" (perhaps a slight exaggeration). [Mrs Ashwell, a childless widow in 1750 moved to Cardigan, died 6 January 1763, buried at St. Mary's.]

The hounding of poor John Laugharne by these sisters and their awful husbands now forms the theme of my story. Laugharne was hardly the man to take things lying down, and immediately after the marriage of Mrs Lilly, carried out some researches into the biography of his newly acquired brother-in-law, and after a time deemed to be possessed of sufficient evidence to upset the legality of the union. Accordingly, in 1736, he prevailed upon Joseph Williams, High Constable of Dewsland [Dewisland], to make a presentation on the Court of Great Sessions against Lilly, alleging that he had committed bigamy. The dancing master had in fact married one Priscilla Earl at Hereford [Cathedral] on 6 February 1726, who, it was claimed, was still living at the time of his marriage to Miss Laugharne, but Lilly was able to how that Priscilla was dead and the court threw out the presentment. [I cannot find any record of Priscilla's death].

Suspecting that Laugharne might take steps to prevent the entail of the estate [endowments, rents etc. left to his wife and daughters by Walter Laugharne], Lilly employed a Carmarthen attorney, Nathaniel Morgan, to enquire into the whole position of the settlements and to submit a case for counsel's opinion on the point. Lilly's suspicions were not unfounded. [John Laugharne on 29 March 1736 had unlawfully granted out several leases on his estate]... This was the initial stage in breaking and barring an entail.' [John Laugharne 'delayed paying portions to his siblings, agreed by his father's deed on 17 April 1715 and will of 1726']. In 1738 John Laugharne [countering Lilly's actions] 'exhibited a Bill of Complaint in the Court of Great Sessions against his mother, sisters, and Mr. Lilly.'

On 9 August 1739, James Lilly was involved in the case against John Laugharne regarding the release of a messuage (dwelling-house with outbuildings) and land called Treyscaw and Clawdd Cam, a water corn grist mill called Llanrithan (sic) Mill. The plaintiffs were 'Elizabeth Laugharn [sic] of Haverfordwest, widow, William Laugharn of Trevach, clerk, Dorothy Laugharn of Haverfordwest, spinster, Margaret Laugharn of the same, spinster, James Lilly of Cardigan, gent and Anne his wife.' (*Bronwydd Estate records file 1461*). The Court ruled that £491. 12s. 6d.; £421. 4s. 6d. and £352. 7s. 10d. (legacies and interest) was due to James and Anne Lilly, Dorothy Laugharne and Margaret Laugharne respectively. The defendant John Laugharne's costs came to £2. 2s. 11d., and the total amounted to £1,285. 7s. 9d., which was to be found by the sale or mortgage of the estate. The decision was confirmed by Order on 8 May 1739. This is an extremely interesting document, as it is signed and sealed by John Laugharne, his mother Elizabeth, his brother William, his sisters Dorothy and Margaret, and by James Lilly and his wife Anne. Dorothy and Margaret Laugharne received £600 from Edward Davies to secure a deed of mortgage, with which they appeared to pay off James and Anne Lilly the monies owed by John Laugharne.

Lilly is described as a 'gentleman' of the town of Cardigan, and on 20 October 1739 we read 'Received this Day of the Date of the within Written Indenture of and from the within named Dorothy Laugharn and Margaret Laugharn the full sum of four hundred ninety one pounds two shillings and sixpence being the consideration money mentioned to be paid to us this day

£491:12:6' It was signed by James and Anne, and significantly one of the three witnesses was John Stokes, whose maid married William Owen. This sum is worth over £70,000 today, but it appears that Lilly was virtually penniless and thieving within a few years.

In 1739/1740, Lilly was living in Cardigan and attempting to trade with Ireland using William Owen's ship, but an embargo meant that Owen was unable to deal in Ireland and he lost money. Thus 'William Owen, Mariner', indicted Lilly, 'late of the Town of Cardigan'. Owen 'complained that of 1 July 1740 at Caron [Lilly] was indebted the Forty Pounds' (c.£3,600 today, *18/272 Cardigan Roll*). The case was heard again in Carmarthen in 1742, with Lilly being associated with Tregaron.

In 1740 John Laugharne recruited tenants to beat back a party of men led by the under-sheriff which was trying to confiscate 30 head of cattle to meet debts. Laugharne made his mansion 'impregnable' against bailiffs but was caught out by a ruse in April 1743. An attractive girl on horseback, Elizabeth David of Roch, was invited into the house by Laugharne by-passing his guards. She asked for a glass of ale, and gave him a letter which she wished him to read for her. Laugharne put it in his pocket, went to get the drink, and on returning found that she had ridden off. Examining the letter, he discovered it was a writ, which was the beginning of the end for him, as he had to answer it.

His sisters had complained against him, and he counter-claimed that Dorothy, then living with her mother at Haverfordwest, had stolen a silver tumbler, six silver spoons and two silver salt cellars from Llanreithan and sold them. This may be the basis of Vincent's story of the robbery at Llanreithan. John Laugharne ignored a summons, so in April 1744 his estates were sequestered, and he went into hiding until the end of 1746. Elizabeth Laugharne, the mother of John, in her will of 2 June 1746 left only one shilling each to her two sons and three daughters, with £5 to be shared between the children of Margaret Essex.

At the Carmarthen Circuit Great Sessions (NLW 14/53, 160) upon 17 August 1744, there was a case against James Lilly. 'Upon motion of Mr Nares and by the consent of Mrs Parry it is ordered that the money delivered her and found on the defendant be delivered by her to the Secondary of this Court for Safe Keeping... [it involved] thirty three Guineas of ye Money was Taken on Lilly at Colton's[?] Inn [Scolton?] and Two Double Johns and Five Single Johns and four Guineas and a Half at St Dogmael's, as appears by the evidence [scrawl] Upon Motion of Mr Davies this [illegible] Cautioning Discontinued.' A Double John was in fact a double Johannes, a Portuguese gold coin, and Portuguese coins were manufactured in, and popular in England. Many were made by John Kirk in London in 1747. After 1762, eleven Portuguese coin weights were standardised, from the double johannes, johannes, moidore and guinea down to the eighth-guinea. The largest coin was worth £3 12s., with a mass of 18dwt (10g), and the guinea worth 21s., with a mass of 5dwt (9g). Thus Lilly was said to be carrying £34 13s in 1744, around £5,200 today. One wonders what Lilly was doing for a living at this time, having had seven children and seemingly having squandered his wife's inheritance.

In March 1745, he was convicted of the 'theft of wearing apparel', two linen shirts, belonging to his brother-in-law, the Reverend William Laugharne, and sentenced to seven years transportation to a plantation in America. Lilly escaped from Haverfordwest gaol where he was awaiting transportation, to join with Lilly practising highway robbery and burglary, being shot dead by Owen in 1747 during a chase by a hue and cry.

By 1 January 1746 OS, i.e. 1747, John Laugharne was in gaol

at Haverfordwest. On 12 July 1748 at the Court of Great Sessions Laugharne was said to be worth £19,000 and keeping armed men. In September 1749, with three men, the Rev. John Davies of Llanreithan beat him up severely. Laugharne went away after more disruption and writs but was back in Llanreithan in 1753, dying in 1755. He still possessed the house and a small part of the estate, and left all to his new wife Mary and baby daughter, the one-year-old Sophie. Laugharne's sisters Mrs Lilly, Mrs Benbow (died without issue) and Mrs Ashwell (died childless in January 1763 in Cardigan) contended that Laugharne had never married Mary, trying to force her out of the house, but it was proved that the marriage was legal.

There seems to be an echo of some of these events in Owen's confession and Vincent's remembrances. The defensive measures of John Laugharne at Llanreithan resemble those of Thomas Johnes at Abermâd.

Chapter 4

The Real Life of William Owen

The following chapter is an attempt to authenticate some of William Owen's claims. When we strip out the bombast and self-regard, there is a strong element of truth in his story, with notable omissions and additions. Certainly the privateering expeditions are difficult to research and validate, for obvious reasons, but much of his history of crime around the British Isles can be substantiated. Owen claims that he was born in Nevern (Nanhyfer), Pembrokeshire, and in January 1717, William, the son of Owen David Bowen, was born in the parish, recorded as '*Gulielmus filius Audoeni David Bowen*'. The entry in the Nevern Parish Register is 10 January 1716, but from 1155 to 1752, the civil or legal year in began on 25 March (Lady Day), so dates before 1752 are referred to as 'Old Style.' This William Owen New Style birth in 1717 thus fitted perfectly with our villain, but fortunately Dr. Reginald Davies discovered that William, son of Owen David Bowen, was buried upon 21 April 1717 (and Jacob, son of Owen David Bowen was buried in June 1718.)

This occurred after many weeks of research into the Owens living in the large hundred of Nevern, which consists of that parish and 27 others. (These comprise Moylegrove, Bayvil, Monnington, St Dogmael's, Llantood, Eglwyswrw, Llanfair-Nant-Gwyn, Llangolman, Llandilo, Eglwyswen/Whitechurch, Meline, Llanfyrnach, Mynachlog-Ddu, Maenclochog, Vorlan, Henry's Moat, Castlebythe, Morvil, Puncheston, Little Newcastle, Pontfaen, Llanychaer, Llanychlwydog, Newport, Llanllawer, Dinas and Fishguard. However, apart from the remarkably complete parish registers of Nevern, there are hardly any extant records available for these surrounding

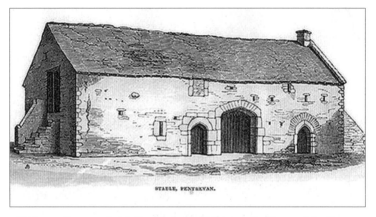

Pentrevan Barn, probably the original hall, the ancestral home of the Owens,
near Pentre Ifan Burial Chamber, Nevern

parishes. Owen never gives us the name of his parents, but
states he had a sister, and that his father was a farmer of
substantial means, as Owen states that his father twice
purchased a sea-going vessel for him. Owen certainly wished
to associate himself with the Owens of the region, one of the
most powerful and notable of all Pembrokeshire families. It was
initially thought that William Owen's birthplace may have been
a former mansion outside Nevern, Pentre Evan (Ifan). He
certainly represents himself as being above the common herd
of people.

Having disposed of the former notion that William was the
son of Owen David Bowen, it was necessary to trawl Nevern
parish registers, as he states he is from Nevern. In adjacent
Eglwyswen, the twins *Gulielmus and Maria filius and filia Thomas*
[Rees?] *Agricola* [farmer] were born on 1 July 1716. William
Owen claims his father was a wealthy farmer, and he had a
sister, but the surname is wrong. For the period 1714-1719, we
only have a record of one William Owen. Upon 29 January 1715,
we read of the baptism of *Gulielmus filius Audoeni John de*

[Tregaman?]. The last word could possibly read Tregarn or some such, but there was a grand house at Tregaman near Nevern, adjoining one of the Owen seats in the parish. However, it is stated that he is thirty years old when condemned, in his 1747 confession transcript, so we shall use a 1717 birthdate. The Reverend Vincent, in his above account, gives a birthplace in St Dogmael's, the parish adjoining Nevern, but the records no longer exist.

According to William Owen's account, his father could afford to send him to school, buy two sea-going trading vessels for him, and intended for William to go to university to become a clergyman. As the only existing universities at this time were Oxford, Cambridge, Glasgow, Aberdeen and Edinburgh, all charging substantial fees, either William's father was indeed wealthy, or William is embellishing the truth. Hating the idea of being a farmer or studying to become a minister or lawyer, William ran away from home, to Haverfordwest, intending a maritime career. For a year his coaster traded from Bristol, but William was treated poorly, whipped and thought himself 'too much of a gentleman for such usage'.

His parents were delighted when he returned to the farm, but William wearied on being 'on a level with the common labourers' and went sailing aboard a Bideford ship. He says he was 'very well-respected having half a man's wage.' Aged perhaps sixteen, he was back at the farm in 1733, and states that his father bought him a small vessel, to stop him running off again. It seems that William was their only son, so his parents pandered to his wishes. However, young William 'betook himself to debauchery' in Cardigan, with a maidservant of Madam Stokes. In anger, his father took back William's boat, and William married the maid, Anne Nicholas, 'out of revenge' at Cardigan on 15 February 1735. William was probably only just eighteen, and the maid was pregnant. Their daughter Ann

Owen was baptised on 9 November 1735, 36 weeks after the wedding. William's father regretted the marriage to a woman of poor means, but returned him his vessel so he could make a living. William Owen only spent a year in legitimate trading, before turning to much more lucrative smuggling activity. However, returning from the Isle of Man, a smuggling haven, his ship was seized by Customs.

Thus around May 1736, young William tells us he enlisted as second mate on the *Joy*, sailing for the West Indies. Quarrelling and wishing to duel with her captain at Barbados, William says he escaped a party of constables who came to arrest him for desertion. William tells us he now boarded the *Terrible* as its mate, and set about organising its defences. In 1736, while smuggling in the Caribbean she was faced by two well-armed Spanish coastguard vessels. His captain wished to flee, but William convinced the crew to fight. According to his account, there ensued a savage two-hour battle, with 25 Spaniards being killed because of his plan of rolling lit gunpowder casks onto the enemy's deck. Another 35 Spaniards died, Owen was wounded in the head, and 11 sailors on the *Terrible* were killed. However, the survivors (especially William) were hailed as heroes on their return to Barbados. The *Terrible* was one of four Liverpool privateers, noted in 1744 as having 22 guns and 180 men under Captain Cole. In 1736, Owen reckons she had 24 guns but only 60 men. In his c.22 months operating out of Barbados, William admits to visiting a brothel, having several affairs, and producing children 'of all colours'.

William states he carried on smuggling, taking 'fighting command' of the *Mayflower*, a vessel owned by New York and Barbados merchants. Making a round voyage to the Bay of Honduras, he took a ship. but fighting off two Spanish coastguard vessels lost six dead and ten wounded before shearing off. Next, as captain of the *Fly*, a well-armed schooner, he attempted to seize a cargo of salt at Salamanca Island, but was again intercepted by a *guarda-costa*, losing four men with five wounded before returning to Barbados. His next voyage in the *Fly* was to smuggle French goods from Martinique to Antigua, followed by a trip back to Martinique to smuggle goods back to Barbados. However, he was intercepted by a 50-gun English man-of-war, *HMS Oxford*. This was around February, 1738. Her captain was extremely pleased with capturing such a noted 'warrior' (– William Owen always praises himself in his account, but does not mention the name of the captain). He made William a midshipman, with the promise of becoming an officer in the navy, and the *Fly* was returned to her owners. This whole episode seems to stretch credulity – it seems far more likely that, as Vincent writes, William was pressed into naval service. However, it is not unknown for pressed men to become midshipmen. Rodger writes that: 'It was quite possible for a good man pressed at sea to step straight into a petty officer's berth, or even straight onto a quarterdeck. Pressed men rated midshipmen, or given warrants, were not unknown, and there was nothing to stop a pressed man rising as high in the service as any other.' With no research carried out in Barbados/the West Indies or the National Maritime Museum, this author has not been able to corroborate any of Owen's privateering on the *Joy*, *Terrible*, *Mayflower* and *Fly*, especially the *Fly's* fight against the *Oxford*.

Next, he served on *HMS Oxford*, which was not 'stationed at Barbados', as Owen writes. Muskett points out that she sailed out of Spithead in March 1736, and her captain died soon after a conflict on the Guinea Coast. Lieutenant Dennison took command, sailing into Carlisle Bay, Barbados on January 29, 1737. Dennison records that the ship stayed for '32 days which time we was employed in victualling, watering and overhauling the rigging.' (*Admiralty papers ADM51*, log of the *Oxford* 29

January 1737). She sailed for Britain on 2 March via the African coast, 'looking at trade with the Europeans'. Thus if he actually served on the *Oxford*, William Owen was probably pressed at Barbados around February 1737, or taken at sea around that time. William says he was honoured going ashore as the 'captain's companion', but the *Oxford's* captain from April 1738 was Thomas Griffin. She arrived in England that month, staying in home waters until August 1739, before sailing in December to cruise off Spain and Portugal before entering the Mediterranean. In February 1739 an Admiralty Commission came aboard at Spithead, and examined 43 men who had signed a petition against Griffin, his 2nd lieutenant and other officers. Griffin does not sound like a man who would have befriended William and given him leave to take up an inheritance. Thus if William was on the *Oxford* it may have been under Dennison. There appears to be no William Owen in the crew lists, but there is at this time a man named Oxford on *HMS Oxford*, which may be Owen's pseudonym, as well as a William Lewis, who may be his faithful lieutenant over the years.

After completing 20 months at sea, we read that a letter from his father eventually reached William upon the *Oxford*, telling him that his second child, William, had been baptised on 30 August 1737. William Owen will have known that the child could not have been his, as he had gone to sea in May 1736. He now forged a letter to be allowed to leave the man-of-war. The *Oxford* was in home waters from December 1738 to June 1739. William tells us he next made land at Portsmouth around November 1739, after three and a half years at sea. Again his indulgent father helped his son, giving William money to buy a vessel, the *Dispatch*, in Swansea in 'Autumn', which must be 1739. On 1 July 1740 there was a court case brought against James Lilly for non-payment of £40. William had probably agreed to freight goods for him but was detained at Dublin by an embargo and trading problems. William was to again sue Lilly two years later. This was the time of the 'Great Frost' and the first Irish Famine of 1840-41, where 38% of the population died. He sold the *Dispatch*, bought the *Blessing* and refitted her. It seems that William Owen was now often operating out of Douglas, Isle of Man, giving him excellent opportunities for smuggling. His trading business succeeded so well that William began malting, and also curing herrings.

Not only in Ireland was there famine. In 1740 there were poor harvests across the rest of the British Isles, with riots across the land and pleas to magistrates for a 'just price' for cereals. Self-appointed 'regulators' would seize outgoing cargoes of wheat and barley and sell at prices the population could afford. While anchored at Cardigan, on 1 March 1741 a gang of 80 men attacked William's ship, the *Blessing*, which may well have been an attempt to stop him sailing with grain for Ireland. William fired over the mob to no effect, so then deliberately wounded a ring-leader. With just two men he tells us that he saw off the chastened attackers, and was informed that the rioters had been given drink to incite them into action, by a local man who had quarrelled with William. In his confession, William totally omits his prosecution against seven of the mob for riotous assembly and stealing his mainsail. William brought an indictment of trespass for riotous assembly against the group of 'disturbors of the peace' in Cardigan against a group who 'riotously and unlawfully who assembled into or upon the sloop or ship called the *Blessing* of Cardigan... the possession of William Owen Master of the same ship did enter and with knives and axes and billhooks and other offensive weapons the sails and riggings of the ship did tear and destroy and one mainsail belonging to the same to the value of Four Pounds with force and arms did take away to the great Damages of the said William Owen esquire...' (*NLW* 814/3)

In the *Bristol Port Book* (E190/1215/3) we see that on 31 July 1741 William seems to be engaged in legitimate trade, as Master of the *Blessing* of Cardigan. His outwards cargo consisted of '20 bends leather, 800 lbs cheese, 9 kilderkins (half barrels) of muscovado sugar, two kilderkins ditto, one roundlet (1/14 of a tun, about 17 gallons) molasses, 1 kilderkin refined sugar, 4 barrels pitch, 2 barrels tar, 1 barrel 2 roundlets train (whale) oil, 1 bag allom (alum), 1 cask 1 bottle English brandy, one roundlet vinegar, 6 boxes and 760 lbs tobacco, 3 kilderkins soap, 1 roundlet vinegar (again), 4 paper parcels starch, 2 boxes soap, 1 box 1 roundlet vinegar, 4 paper parcels, 2 boxes soap, 20 reams paper, 5 casks 1 bottle olive oil, 1 roundlet vinegar, 1 cask brandy.'

Regarding the attack by the mob at Cardigan, Parry tells us 'the Cardigan Grand Jury returned a true bill at the Cardigan Spring Great Sessions of 1742 but the verdict is not known (*NLW, Great Sessions 4/892/4*). This does not square up to Owen's assertion that he "made a peace with them [the rioters]" since prior to the formation of a professional police force prosecutions were almost invariably instigated by individuals.' At the Sessions, William was bound over to keep the peace, especially towards the mariner John Bowen of St. Dogmael's. Parry informs us: 'As John Bowen heads the seven names on the indictment of the rioters so that it is quite probable that he was the "chief" – as Owen calls him – whom he shot.' The National Library of Wales *Crime and Punishment* website gives us details of the men. All the attackers were from St Dogmael's, just across the River Teifi from Cardigan, charged with 'Food riot and destroying the sails of prosecutor's ship – The Blessing'. They were John Bowen, mariner; William John, ship carpenter; Joshua Lewis, joiner; George Lloyd, mariner; David William Morris, yeoman; Thomas William Morris, yeoman; and John Rowland, carpenter. [*NLW 814/3*]. The cause of the trouble may well have been a food riot opposing the export of corn, just a year after poor harvests and terrible food shortages had provoked riots across England and Wales. Outward shipments of grain were even confiscated by magistrates to be sold cheaply to local people.

In the Court of Great Sessions of March 1742 (*NLW 4/892/4*) we read 'James Lilly late of the Town of Cardigan in the County of Cardigan was entailed to answer William Owen Mariner in a plea of trespass... and whereupon the said William Owen by Thomas Lloyd his Attorney complains that whereas the said James Lilly upon the first day of July in the year of our Lord Jesus Christ 1740 at Caron in the County of Cardigan aforesaid was indebted to the said William Owen in the Sum of Forty Pounds of Good and Lawful Money of Great Brittain for the Work and Labour of the said William for him the said James at his Special Instance and Request of him the said James...' There follows a long repetitious transcript, ending with asking James Lilly, by Jacob his Attorney, to come and defend himself. In Ceredigion, 'Caron uwch Clawdd' is Ystrad Fflur (Strata Florida, on Sarn Helen and the River Teifi) and 'Caron is Clawdd' on the Teifi is Tregaron. Both are referred to as 'Caron' in early documents and census returns including 1891.

On 14 June 1742 a mob of Llanychaearn and Llanilar yeomen, probably all tenants of the Abermâd estate, were led by 'a Llanbadarn gentleman and John Johnes of Llanychaearn, gentleman', to attack the attorney Thomas Parry's house in Aberystwyth. Windows were smashed, with threats being made to demolish the house and to kill Parry. The Johnes family of Abermâd had around 40 men and kept harassing Parry, whose Llidiardu estate at Llanilar neighboured Abermâd. Cardiganshire records demonstrate that local gentry often used violence against their enemies, and Thomas Johnes rivalled his contemporary and enemy, Herbert Lloyd of Peterwell (see *The*

Cwilt Conundrum, chapter 7) in his acts of menace. Parry had brought an action of debt against Thomas Johnes, the High Sheriff of Cardigan from 1737, in April 1741. Johnes consistently refused to appear in court, and the suit and damages were awarded to Parry. The haughty Johnes was in financial distress, and is said to have forced messengers to eat any summonses. Johnes had mortgaged his estate in 1736, and then refused to pay the interest on the mortgage, even though proceedings 'were taken again and again'. They failed because 'Thomas Johnes had lived many years past in open and publick defiance of the law' (– *NLW, Great Sessions 18/272*).

In his account, in 1742 William helped his friend Thomas Parry, an Aberystwyth attorney, in a retaliatory attack on Thomas Johnes' great house at Abermâd. Thomas Johnes had around 40 followers, always armed, and cannon mounted on top of his mansion. William, calling himself 'General Owen', besieged the house, and after an 11-hour siege, forced Johnes to surrender. In 1757, Thomas Johnes was finally imprisoned for debt, in the Fleet, London, languishing there for three years. (Johnes features strongly in the lawlessness of Herbert Lloyd, described by Bethan Phillips in *Peterwell*). The attack by William could well have happened, but the fortification of the manor and defiance of authority is replicated in the story of John Laugharne of Llanreithan, in the account of James Lilly's life. The event seems unrecorded, but Parry writes: 'Incredible as this attack sounds, on the mansion house of a man who was, after all, High Sheriff of Cardiganshire in 1752, it is authenticated by strong circumstantial evidence.'

William now smuggled goods around Ireland, the Isle of Man, north-west England, Scotland and Wales, encountering Customs officers and storms. The port ingates record from 19 February 1742 (Old Style) has to be amended to 1743 (New Style – from 1155 to 1752, the civil or legal year in England began on 25 March, Lady Day, not 1 January.) Thus on 19 February 1743 we read that 'Wm Owen Enters off Board the *Blessing* himself Master from Waterford.' His cargo was two carcasses of beef, 400 cwt of butter and 400cwt of 'tallow vat' (rendered beef or mutton fat), upon which he only paid 4½ pence in duty. Owen refitted his *Blessing* as the *Prince Charles*, and smuggled herring to Waterford, taking on goods for the Isle of Man. He then took

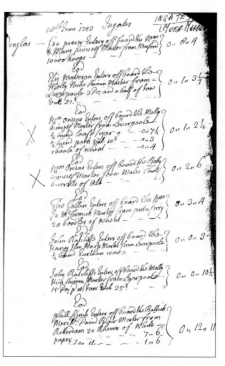

19 February 1742 (– 1743 N.S.)

contraband to Liverpool, purchasing swivel guns and armaments for his ship. Owen next accounts that he smuggled to Westmorland and Cumberland, pretended to be a Welsh gentleman and then a Scottish pedlar, and disposed of silks and tea in Liverpool.

The Whitehaven Customs Collector and Controller wrote that the sloop *Prince Charles* of Beaumaris put into the port on 17 February 1743 and was boarded and searched, after 'information' about her had been received. A more thorough search was carried out three days later, because the ship's master had failed to report to the Custom House. The report of the Collector of Whitehaven to the Board (*CUST82/4*) reads:

th side of this Harbour, & it was with great difficulty
y regained it, about eleven that night when the tide
ebb was made, the Collector went down to the low key
offered twelve shillings to two boats to endeavour to
get her out, but they would not undertake it upon wch
ordered the Capt to try in the morning & that he &
the Tidesurveyor would meet him at Workington by land
the next tide the wind coming more favourable, the
sloop got under sail afloat as she was afloat &
nced Lewis at sea about a league to the seaward,
ring before the wind as fast as he cad crowd, about
the Kings sloop came near him when Lewis fired
great Guns, one of wch went thro his foresail & the
her pass'd near his mainmast, Capt Robinson return'd
he fire upon wch Lewis gave them another broad side
cut their rigging & then hauled up his sails & laid by
telling them, he & his crew were resolved all to die
rather than be taken & so they all retir'd into close qrs
yt Mr Robinson's hands knew she was well provided
with, having eight loop holes out of the cabbins bea...
to clear the deck with & their powder being near spent
they refus'd to board her, & left her, upon wch Lewis
made sail to the westward, she is a painted sloop with
a white bottom, a small horse head about 18 or 20 Tons
six swivel Guns upon her cabbin head or quarter deck ten
of them of wood, two large brass Guns, 3 case of Pistol
besides cutlashes & other small arms, 8 loop holes out
of the cabbin to the deck, 4 more into the hold...

The official account of Owen's action against the Revenue Cutter off Workington 1 March 1743

'On the 17th inst a small sloop came into this harbour, she was haled as she passed the pierhead by the Tidesurveyor and answered from Lancaster with empty casks, the surveyor sent his boat on board, the master said she was called the *Prince Charles* of Beaumaris, that she came from thence with herrings to Lancaster & was come hither for coals and that his name was Joshua Lewis the boatmen after a slight rummage finding nothing but empty casks left her, Lewis not coming to the Custom house the said surveyor on the 20 went on board with his crew, & on rummaging the hold more carefully than had been done before, found forty pounds of tea in papers in an empty herring cask and two papers more in the cabbin drawers, Lewis who had two pistols on the table and was loading a third, said he had met with the tea at sea...' William, calling himself Joshua Lewis, had two pistols primed and was loading another, and said first that he had come across the tea at sea, and then altered his story and said that he had brought it from Lancaster, so it was not contraband. He was told to present his papers to the Customs House, but sailed off that night.

The Collector discovered that bad weather had forced William to shelter off Workington and ordered the *Sincerity* to take 'Joshua Lewis', but contrary winds prevented her sailing. Two tidesmen and a boatman had been sent overland to join with Workington officers and take William, but 'Lewis, seeing them come down the river in the King's boat brought his crew upon deck with lighted matches, pointed his guns into the boat, swore he would sink her if they attempted to board him, his men were armed with cutlasses and small arms & he had several pistols in his belt, the officers having no arms, retir'd and sent us notice.' Held back by adverse winds, three days later William was approached off Workington, by Captain Robinson in the heavily armed and well-manned revenue cruiser *Sincerity*. It carried 18 men, 6 carriage guns and 8 swivel guns. The *Sincerity* caught up with the *Prince Charles*, whereupon according to what Robinson told the Collector, 'Joshua Lewis' 'fired his great guns [i.e. cannon] one of which went through his [Robinson's] foresail and the other passed near his mainmast'. It seems that Robinson fabricated the notion that William had cannon aboard. He returned a broadside, but another broadside from William cut the *Sincerity's* rigging. 'Lewis, gave them another broadside which cut their rigging and then hauled up his sails and laid by telling them, he and his crew were resolved all to die, rather than be taken & so they all retired into close quarters, which Mr Robinson's hands knew she was well provided with, having eight loop holes out of the cabbin's breasting, to clear the deck with & their powder being near spent they refused to board her, and left her.'

Robinson strangely ran out of powder after just one

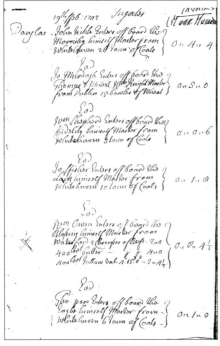

12 June 1743

broadside, or was covering for his, and his crew's cowardice. William Owen, aka Joshua Lewis, sailed off westward. William's sloop was described as 'a painted sloop with a white bottom a small horse head about 18-20 tons, with six swivel guns upon her cabbin deck or quarter deck, two of them wood, two large brass guns, 3 case of pistols besides cutlasses & other small arms, 8 loop holes out of the cabin to the deck, 4 more into the hold – is square sterned, carrys 5 hands.' (*TNA, Customs Outport Records, Collector to Board, Whitehaven, CUST82/3*, 26 February 1743). The report goes on to identify Joshua Lewis as 'Owens', 'said to belong to Aberdovey, Beaumaris or some other port in Wales, trades often to the Isle of Man, has always a number of empty casks about herring gauge in her hold by way of a cloke [cloak] as we have since heard & that she was formerly a pleasure boat built by a gentleman in Wales, and Lewis to prevent any umbrage being taken at his guns & arms gives out that he wants to sell them.' William now relates that he sailed the *Prince Charles* to the Isle of Man on 2 March 1743, being treated 'as if he were their prince', while the *Sincerity* made it back to

Whitehaven 'in a shattering condition.' Estranged from his adulterous wife, which was truly a case of 'the pot calling the kettle black', he fell in love with a young Manx girl, and they passed themselves off as man and wife.

He may well have 'married' around now, bigamously. Man's governor later wrote that he thought Owen had married around early January 1743. William later took refuge on Man with Edward Christian, along with his Manx 'wife', probably Mary Kelly. Despite her misgivings, he smuggled brandy, rum, tobacco, tea and silks to South Wales, and said he was asked to help turn in salt smugglers, which he used as a cover to sell his cargo.

Upon 8 June 1743, in the report of the Collector of Whitehaven, there is 'an affidavit of the obstruction several officers were met with from Joshua Lewis otherwise Owen in the Execution of our orders to stop his Sloop, sworn before the Collector a Commissioner in the court of Kings bench – William Roberts master of a vessel at Carnarvon informs us that he is well acquainted with the above person who they look upon as a Sort of Pirate in Wales & that his true name is William Owen. (*CUST82/4*, 8 June 1743). The Douglas ingates record for 10 June 1743 is 'Wm Owens Enters Off Board the *Molly* himself Master from Liverpool: ½ hund loaf of sugar 7½d; ½ hund pork vat 3d; 1 bowl of wheat 4d, paying duty of 1s 2½d. The entry below is Wm Owens Enters off Board the *Betty* himself Master from Wales 2 half barrells of Ale – 3s 4d.'

He states that around this time he landed at St Bride's, and fought with the Irish smuggler Patrick Donohaws (it seems to be originally spelt Donahaws) of Wexford near Fishguard, but this author can as yet find no person with a similar name in the contraband trade at this time. Finding his wife 'dead drunk' in Cardigan, William paid off her debts and denounced her. She had borne a son which was not his, and he said he wished to 'marry' his young Manx lady. Disaster now struck in Westmorland, where William landed at Grange-over-Sands and made for Kendal to make arrangements to sell smuggled cargo, but his ship was taken by Customs, involving the loss of both the *Prince Charles* and £400-£500 worth of goods (around £70,000 today). The treacherous Yorkshireman he had left in charge of the cargo was shot in the hand by William Lewis. William made for Lancaster, and Captain Frazer reunited William with his young lady. They temporarily separated, as she went to Liverpool to stay with relatives and William managed to procure a cow and raffle it for thirty guineas. With William Lewis again, he settled his debts and bought horses to return to Liverpool and sailed for Douglas, Isle of Man.

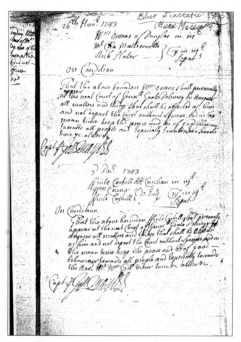

Summons at Douglas Isle of Man, 26 November 1743 regarding Owen

Penniless, he joined a Manx ship, smuggling goods to Liverpool, North Wales and Cumberland in November 1743, and then a large quantity of tea to Barmouth. There is an interesting report in the Manx Museum (*Lib Scacc*, 26 November 1743) regarding 'William Owens of Douglas': 'On Condition That the above Bounden Wm Owens shall personally appear at the next Court of General Gaole Delivery to Answer all matters and things that shall be objected against him and not depart the Court without Lycence and in the mean time keep the peace and be of good behaviour towards all people and especially towards John Kinsale.' From Man he sailed for Liverpool with tea, then on a Manx boat to Duddon, Cumberland as pilot, then to Barmouth, selling goods in Chester.

Using money from his new 'wife', William sailed to Conwy to purchase a yacht from a local squire. It seems that the money came from other sources. Muskett reveals that the boat sale was on 4 February 1744, but on 1 February William Owen had sold a quarter share to John Callow for ten pounds. Other transactions around this time meant that William owned less than a quarter of the sloop. John Callow was one of William Owen's crew, who made over his share to Phillip Moore, the

In February 1744, Owen bought a yacht off Edward Pugh of Penrhyn Old Hall, Conwy

brother of a prominent merchant George Moore, who supplied the smuggling trade. The sloop *James and Bridget* was bought from Edward Philip Pugh, who lived at what is now Penrhyn Old Hall, and was Sheriff of North Wales in 1743. The building, dating from the 14th century, is now a pub on the outskirts of Llandudno. In 1760 it passed from the family to Dr. John Williams, Archbishop of York and Keeper of the Great Seal. (A 'yacht' at this time was a 'pleasure boat', the term remembered in the royal 'yacht' *Britannia*. In 1750 yachts were defined as having 'one mast with a halfspreet or smack sail, and sometimes ketch fashion.' A 1791 Manx yacht, *Peggy*, has recently been restored). William Owen immediately added to its armoury, loaded the *James and Bridget* with contraband and sailed for St Bride's Bay, Pembroke to sell off most of the cargo.

On 12 March 1744 William Owen sailed once more into Cardigan, and fought off a revenue cruiser by firing a broadside. He then moored his vessel, and distributed the remaining cargo, unloading it alongside the Customs House. Hugh Morgan, Collector of Customs, discovered that Owen was in port and organised an armed party to bring him in, including bailiff's men, and James Moss, a deserter from the 34th Regiment of Foot held in Cardigan Gaol. In all there were around 20 men – 4 Spanish prisoners-of-war, 2 convicts, a tide-officer, 'catch poles' (officers employed to make arrests) and 'informers'. Moss was later to give a first-hand account of the affair. The party marched to attack Owen at 4 am, with one of the Spaniards being told to shoot him in his bed. Owen's vessel, the *Blessing*, was beached with the tide out, and on 4 April 1744 James Phillips, a Customs boatman leading the party, charged Owen with outlawry, as he had 'lately fired at the King's Boat when it was coming on board him'. William replied that 'his Vessel was his Castle' and offered ale and ten guineas to be left in peace. William refused and shot Phillips dead from his cabin.

Moss and the others shot down into William's cabin, but the returning fire was too great, and after deaths and injuries, Owen was left in peace.

William and his crew killed 2 Spaniards and 2 Welshmen, one of whom was the Customs Officer. William Lewis shot James Moss, a deserter from the 33rd Regiment of Foot, who was imprisoned and thrown in the forecastle for three days, and later made a full deposition of the night's events. Hugh Morgan confirmed than three men died of gunshot wounds, one dying after William put him ashore, but he took the injured Moss as a prisoner. One Spaniard drowned. As soon as the weather was fine, four days later, he sailed off for the Isle of Man. As well as his faithful aide William Lewis and Robert Calcot, there were two Manx smugglers aboard the *Blessing*, William Carron (Carroune, Carran) and John Callowe (Curlow, Callow, Carlow).

Bridge over the Teifi at Cardigan leading from St Dogmael's to the castle

The coroner's inquest found that William Owen, 'mariner' had murdered 'James Phillipps [sic], excise officer by shooting him with a musket in his belly.' The prosecutor was Thomas Griffith, the parish was St Dogmael's, and the offence dated 4 March 1744 upon the *NLW Crime and Punishment* website, but it must be 4 April (*NLW file* 4/814/1). On 4 April 1744, John Rees (aka Rice), the Cardigan coroner, brought together an inquest jury for Domingo do [sic] Zioneto, a Spanish prisoner of war, enquiring 'by what means he came to his death ... upon the ship of William Owen... [he] boarded the said ship with several others and was killed on board the said William Owen out of his cabbin by a person or persons unknown and the jurors further said Murder was committed by the other way.'

NLW File 4/894 of 1744 tells us 'The Judges do present that William Owen late of the Town of Cardigan, the fourth day of April in the seventeenth year of our Sovereign Lord George the Second... notoriously and with malice aforethought at the Parish of St Dogmael's, in the County of Pembroke aforesaid in and upon one James Phillips Gentleman an Officer of His Majesty's Customs in the Execution of his Office... an assault and the said William Owen then and there having a Gun or Muskett in his hands Charged with Powder and leaden balls shott and discharged the same upon the said James Phillips, whereby he gave the said James Phillips one mortall wound on the left side of his belly and through the same [obliterated] of the breadth of two [illegible]. James Phillips Instantly Dyed...' The jury unanimously agreed that Owen 'before thought voluntarily and maliciously did Kill and Murder [James Phillips]'.

Owen asked the captured Moss not to betray him, and let him free on Man, but Moss informed on Owen to Peter Sidebotham, the Customs Surveyor on the Isle of Man. On 28 April, Moss made a full report before Man's Deputy Governors,

John Taubman and Daniel Mylrea about the multiple murders including a Customs Officer. The officials upon that date sent out orders to all the Captains of towns and parishes to bring in Owen, John Callow and Robert Calcot, and ordered all boat owners not to take them off the island. (*Lib Scacc* 28 April 1744). John Taubman was one of the island's chief magistrates, one of two 'deemsters', who were also deputy governers, and also 'one of the Island's major dealers in contraband' (– Muskett).

James Moss had been detained in Cardigan Gaol for theft. He stated that when the party was on the road heading for Owen's ship, it was agreed that one of the Spaniards was to be sent to shoot Owen in his bed. William writes that the men boarded his ship at 4 in the morning, cutting rigging, throwing guns overboard and stealing. When he tried to reason, he was threatened with a pistol and a Spaniard slashed at him with a cutlass, making him beg for his life. With the incoming tide, the *James and Bridget* lifted off, and a firefight ensued. His crew escaped, leaving William Owen and William Lewis shooting from cover, killing four and wounding several others.

Moss testified that William Owen castigated his crewman William 'Carrowns' as an 'Irish dog' for his cowardice in fleeing. Another crew member, 'John Callowe or Curlow', was arrested in Liverpool in August 1744 and examined by its Collector, Mr Colquhoun. At Douglas, William Owen said he paid for Moss to have surgery, but in Liverpool in November 1744 Moss could not be sent to London as a potential witness against William, as 'he was under the surgeon's hand in order to get one of the balls out of his thigh, which gave him a good deal of pain, which he has done and is now able to travel' (– R.C. Jarvis). Another named member of Owen's crew at Cardigan was Robert Calcot.

The *London Gazette* (8-12 May 1744) reported: 'for the better discovery of bringing to Justice the Persons who committed the said Murders, [His Majesty] is pleased to promise his most gracious Pardon to any of them who were on board the said Owen's Sloop (except the Persons who actually committed the said Murders, or either of them) who shall discover his accomplice or accomplices so as they may be apprehended and convicted thereof and as a further encouragement reward of £100 to any who shall discover and apprehend the said William Owen or any other of the offenders to be paid by the Receiver General of His Majesty's Customs upon Conviction 12 May.'

The Duke of Newcastle, Secretary of State and First Lord of the Treasury, personally asked the Duke of Atholl, Lord of Man, to take Owen, and he gave instructions for the crew's arrests. Atholl benefited from the customs duties he imposed on Man, which were a fraction of the sums taken by the Crown on goods entering Britain, and the Isle of Man had been a smuggling haven and sanctuary. However, Owen and his crew had murdered a Customs Officer, and Atholl had no desire for a quarrel with England over a non-Manx national. The Isle of Man's Governor, George Lindesay, wrote that Sidebotham had made such a 'noise' about the island that Owen, Callow and Calcot had escaped on an Irish boat, but Lewis and 'Carron' had been imprisoned in Castle Rushen gaol. Lewis and Carron had applied to be taken on Captain Wickham's HMS Lark on 12 June, and her captain was willing to take them, but the gravity of the crime persuaded Newcastle that they should face trial. There had been a 1744 Proclamation announcing a pardon for all smugglers if they joined the Royal Navy before 20 June 1744, dated 9 May.

William Owen was now wanted for trial for the possible murder of John Hughes, Domingo de Zioneto and James Phillipps, with Pintado's drowning being his own fault. Patrick Lindesay, Governor of the Isle of Man issued a warrant for William Owen's arrest. Owen sailed from Douglas to Peel, but William Lewis and William 'Carroun' were arrested and taken to Castle Rushen. The *James and Bridget* was impounded, and the governor was furious that Owen had escaped.

On 30 April 1744 Governor Lindesay wrote to the Duke of Newcastle regarding 'one William Owen a famous Welsh Runner Outlawed some time ago for killing some of the Revenue Officers in the north of England. [I cannot find a trace of this incident as yet]. This Gentleman had his Vessel well armed it seems went lately to the Coast of Wales [to] run his Goods near Cardigan. An officer was sent aboard, assisted by at least twenty men, most of them prisoners purposely taken out of the Goale there to take him and his Vessel – whereupon a Squabble ensued and the Officers etc. killed as your Grace will see fully by the information enclosed [Moss's deposition].' Lindesay writes that Owen removed to Peel, having known via Sidebotham's indiscretions that he was a wanted man, and 'took the Opportunity of secreting himself so that they could not find him.'

Searches were carried out across Man, and on 1 May the inn of Edward Christian was investigated. Christian's wife was the aunt of Owen's 'wife', and were later disingenuous in their response to the authorities after Owen and his wife stayed there a few weeks later. After hiding in caves from a man-hunt, William and his 'wife' managed to escape in a Strangford oyster-boat, then in May 1744 fled inland from Downpatrick to Lurgan, Armagh, Northern Ireland. The couple pretended to be pedlars (peddlers) for three months at markets and fairs, then returned to Douglas, Isle of Man.

On 18 July 1744, the coroner John Rees brought another inquisition regarding the events of 4 April, with a different jury. 'John Hughes went on board the ship of William Owen... having boarded the said ship with several others, was shot in the thigh on board the said William Owen, out of his cabbin, by a person or persons unknown and that his death came by the other way.'

John Hughes was a Cardigan saddler, and was registered as having been murdered by person(s) unknown, as was Domingo de Zioneto, a Spanish prisoner of war (– the parish was Cardigan, and the prosecutor is unspecified, file *NLW 4/893/1*).

On 2 August 1744, the fourth and final inquisition was held regarding 4 April 'at the house of John Rees, coroner in the town of Cardigan on Thursday the second day of August upon the body of Alfredo Pintado then and there lying dead... the said Alfredo Pintado went on board a ship of William Owen, late of the parish of Cardigan ... then lying in the River Tivy with the Officer of the Customs, pursuant to an information given them and the said Alfredo Pintado having boarded ship with several others, the said got over the side of the said ship and grappled there to save himself from the said William Owen, and was drowned, and that his death came by the other way as with of own hands'. (– *NLW, Great Sessions 4/893/1*). Rees always signed his coroner's reports as John Rice.

In Autumn Sessions of 1744, the Cardiganshire Grand Jury returned a true bill against William Owen, but he could not be tried for felony in absentia, and proceedings were stayed. For the murder of James Phillips, Walter Lloyd, the Attorney-General recommended that there be no further prosecution for the indictment, and it was later decided that Owen would be tried at Hereford. Incidentally, at the Carmarthen Circuit Great Sessions (*NLW 14/53*, 160), upon 17 August 1744, there was also a case against James Lilly, involving over £5,000 in today's money being carried by him, and seemingly the property of Mrs Parry.

After escaping from Peel to Ireland and several adventures, Governor Lindesay was advised that Owen was back on the island on 5 August. Owen and his wife sought shelter at Edward Christian's public house at Onchan near Douglas on 29 August. Edward Christian had married Mary Kelly at Onchan on 21

January 1709, and William's wife was a niece of one of the Kellys in the Island. (The Christian family was still farming at Onchan, just north of Douglas, in the early nineteenth century.) Our Edward Christian may have been born around 1687, being buried at Onchan on 28 June 1766, at an estimated age of 79. Mary Kelly, the daughter of John and Margaret Kelly, and quite possibly William Owen's 'wife', was baptised at St Mathew's, Douglas, on 11 September 1724. Around 1743 Owen he says his 'wife' is around 18 years of age, with several good houses in Douglas. While previously staying with the Christians, Owen went by the name of Cumings, and the family believed that

Castle Rushen, Man, where William Owen was confined in September 1744 before being taken to Liverpool, then Hereford, for trial

there had been a marriage ceremony between him and his Kelly wife. Upon information received, Governor Lindesay sent troops to take the couple, but seeing them coming, Owen escaped through a back door on 5 September 1744.

Mr and Mrs Christian and their daughter were taken into custody for sheltering the couple. Confined at Castle Rushen, 'Edward Christian Senior of Beemanghad [Bemahague], Kirk Conchan [Onchan], Sheading of Garff' made a petition 'for Entertaining one William Owens, which happened by one Evans a Welshman had brought a Stranger to your Petitioner's house after he was in Bed and Called himself by the name of Cumins who Stayed a Night or two at your petitioners who being Busy about his harvest did not know it was Owens till the Soldiers came to his House... and as he is Intirely Innocent Thereon that he may be released to take Care of his harvest...' Upon examination he said that on 29th August the Welshman Evans brought 'William Owens (by having his wife who is a mancks woman along with him) came to the petitioners house about an hour or two of night. That the petitioners wife provided a Bed for the said Owen and wife & they lived there till Monday after – and then he went abroad to Peele – Tuesday morning he returned to the petitioners house – That night or the night after he went to Douglas & came back the same night he went – and continued at the petitioners house till Wednesday last – the petitioner saw him at Dinner that day and Dined with him & his wife & going about his affairs. The Captain & Soldiers came in search of him – The petitioner further saith That he never heard the sd Owen was proclaimed at the parish Churches – but that he knew he had been hunted & searched for in the Island about the beginning of May last or the latter end of April last and that his the petitioners own house was then searched for him – That he knew him before he marryd his sd wife – and hath known him since – And tho' he went under the name of Cumings [sic] when he came this last time to the petitioners house, yet he soon after coming knew him to be Owens.'

This appears to confirm Owen's bigamy. He was known as Owen or Owens in Man, and also as Cumins or Cumings. Edward's wife Mary was also examined, stating that 'altho' the sd Owen went by the name of Cumings This Informant from her knowledge of him before knew him to be Wm Owens – That after some days he went to Peele and came back again – and sometimes went to Douglas & returned – That he Dined with the Informant on Wednesday last before the Capt & Soldiers came but spying them from a Window, made his Escape from the house [5 September] – That the Informant never heard he was proclaimed at the parish Churches, but saith that their house was Searched for him the 1st day of May last.'

The daughter Mary Christian said that Evans brought Owen and his wife to her father's house, and she knew Owen although 'he went under another name' and repeats her parents' story, saying that Owen left the house and never returned but crucially 'his wife is still there.' The two Christian sons, anxious to see their parents released, also informed that William's wife was still in the house, and that he would probably return at night. Accordingly he was ambushed on 7 September and taken to join his two crew mates in Castle Rushen gaol. Callow had been taken in Liverpool the previous day, and gave an anodyne account of the murders, in that Owen was defending himself against Spaniards 'in the night time with drawn cutlasses' in their hands, and that Owen... threatened to fire on them if they did not go ashore.'

On 10 September 1744, George Lindesay reported from Castletown to Lord Atholl at Blair Castle (*Atholl Archive AA[17]42*) that he had received information that Owen had returned to Man, and was concealed in a public house. This information may well have come from one of the Kellys – it appears Owen's wife's family disliked him. He stated that Owen had made an escape as he was standing on a height on 5 September, and saw soldiers approaching. 'Upon this I sent for the master of the house, & committed him prisoner to the Castle, after I had examined him, I found the simple old man knew little of the matter, But that Owen had been entertained by his wife, who is aunt to a young woman, whom Owen had married about nine months ago. [This would make Owen's bigamous marriage around January 1743.]

I therefore sent for the Old Woman & her daughter, who prevaricated a little in their examinations; I also seized the Welsh boat which had brought him, and I believe was to have carried him back had he not been discovered, as the Master of the Boat himself in part owned upon his examination. I likewise embargoed all our own boats, to prevent his getting off the Island'. He also gave orders to militia captains on 6 September 1744 to search and watch the coast and offered a reward of £100 on Owen's head. 'But I found the securing of the old man [probably aged around 57], his wife & daughter had the desired effect, (they are now at liberty upon bail) for his two sons, – who are strong active fellows, finding their family in distress on Owen's account, And that it was almost impossible for him after such precautions, to get of[f] the Island; they informed young Mr Oats whose father is the Captain of that parish company, that Owen's wife was still at their house & they imagined he himself might return in the night time. Accordingly these two, and Mr Oats, who took several others whom he could trust to assist him, laid watch in several places, and surprised and took Owen last Saturday about midnight as he was making a signal to his wife on the outside of the house, & brought him in prisoner to this castle upon Sunday morning the 9th where he is now in Irons in the inner ward. – I am told he behaves with great coolness, said to those who took him that he was not afraid to come of at his trial; But told them solemnly that they were sure of £100 for this job, for he had seen himself advertised in the *Gazette* when he was last at Dublin with £100 premium at his tail.' Lindesay sent his report to the Liverpool Collector of Customs to forward to the Commissioners of Customs in London, for an order to take Owen, Lewis and 'Caronn' off the island, along with James Moss, with 'material evidence', who 'made the first discovery.'

On 27 September, at the Exchequer Court at Castle Rushen, Edward Christian was fined £10 (£1,500 today) for 'contempt and misdemeanour' in harbouring the criminal William Owen for several days and nights 'in a private Clandestine manner', and setting an 'evil example' despite the reward offered. The governor now wanted the prisoners out of the island, and a King's Messenger, John Robson was ordered to take the prisoners William Owen, Lewis, Carroun and the important witness James Moss to England or Wales for trial. On 9 October, William Lewis and William Carroun tried to take advantage of an amnesty for smugglers, and join Captain John Wickham's *HMS Lark*, but the offer did not extend to murderers.

No-one was prepared to help Robinson sail the *Sincerity* into Cardigan, as in Liverpool he found it impossible to engage a pilot. A letter to William Wood dated 2 October 1744 reads: 'every Body expects Owen to be rescued, he being the King of the Smuglers & there is such Numbers of them that every Man that knows the Country is afraid to go among them on this Occasion, besides which we are informed that there is 30 of them gone from the Isle of Man with a Number of fire Arms to join the others in Wales to rescue him so that I apprehend there will be no Probability to convey them by Sea to that part of the Country for he has been there since he committed the Murther

& arm'd his Friends in case of being taken'. (*State Papers SP36/64/348*, 26 October 1744). James Moss was still being treated by a surgeon for his injuries in November 1744.

On 6 October 1744, the Duke of Newcastle wrote to Atholl and Lindesay to deliver Owen, Lewis and William Carron (his name is spelt variously) to the custody of the King's Messenger John Robson. On 8 October Robson acknowledged the order to carry the prisoners 'to Cardigan to be tried for the Murther whereof they stand Charges as Pirates by his Grace the Duke of Newcastle's Warrant for that purpose.' James Moss was meant to be the main witness against Owen, but was threatened by 'some villainous smugglers from the Isle of Man' so did not wish to testify, or be returned to his regiment and whipped for desertion. A Liverpool surgeon was trying to extract the musket ball in his thigh, shot by William Lewis, when a summons to appear in London was sent by the Customs Board. However, seemingly en route, he was captured by a sergeant from his regiment, who 'sent him in irons to Chester gaol' as a deserter.

Upon 12 October the *Sincerity* arrived at Cardigan Bay carrying

Hereford Trial Transcript March 1745

the prisoners, but in bad conditions Captain Robinson could not trust the prisoners to pilot him into harbour. In rising winds, it was decided to sail for Liverpool or Beaumaris, but the ship was forced into Dublin until the storm abated. He sailed into Liverpool on 24 October, Owen having been in custody since 9 September. John Robson, a King's Messenger, an official courier who served warrants, brought Owen and his crew from Liverpool, where they had been held for some months. They were now taken to Hereford for trial, instead of Cardigan. The Commissioners of Customs knew that smugglers were particularly popular in coastal communities, and had a better chance of a guilty verdict in land-locked Hereford. William states that his oratory deeply impressed the judge and gentry. The details of the killed differ from the Cardigan inquest. William and two of his crew, William Lewis and John Callow were charged with the murder of James Phillips and Domingo St. Sebastian (Domingo de Zioneto). All three were acquitted of killing Domingo St. Sebastian, but although acquitted of the murder of Phillips, as William Owen states, they were actually convicted of manslaughter.

At Hereford the charge reads: 'For the Willful Murder of James Philipps one of his Majestyes Custom house Officers in the Execution of in the Execution of his Office the sd. Wm. Owens with a Certain Gun Charged with Gun powder & leaden Sluggs to and against the sd. James Philips did discharge & shot of giving to the sd. James Philips one Mortal wound on the Left side of his Belly of the breadth of one Inch and of the Depth of 10 Inches of which wound he instantly dyed & the sd. William Lewis & John Callow being present and aiding abetting & assisting the sd. Wm. Owens to Comitt the sd. Murder on the fourth day of April in the 17th Year of his present Majesty G.2 at the Drogmeales in the County of Pembroke.' (Although William Owen was indicted he is spelt as Owens, and the spelling of Phillips varies also). The indictment for the murder of Domingo St Sebastian is almost identical, even the description of the wound, but its point of entry is left blank, and Drogmeales becomes Drogwells.

The sentence is unknown, but William Owen states that he went to the Isle of Man immediately after the trial. He may have paid a fine, or it was thought that his six months in prison in Man, Liverpool and Hereford was sufficient punishment. Parry points out that the trial was held on 16 March 1745, not 23 March as Owen stated. William Owen stated that he and his wife went back to Man, where there was 'great rejoicing.' William Lewis carried on working with his long-time master, Owen.

Douglas Ingates 22 June 1745

In March 1745, James Lilly was convicted of the 'theft of wearing apparel'. We do not know the indictment, as the file is missing. *NLW file 14/52* reads 'Whereas James Lilly late of [space left blank] in the said County of Pembroke was at this time in the present Great Sessions, convicted of felony for the felonious taking of two Linnen Shirts of ye Value of three

Shillings and Sixpence of ye propper goods of William Laugharne the Court doth give sentence that he shall be forthwith be transported for Seven Years to Some or One of His Majesty's plantations in Amorica [sic].' It is not known why William Laugharne, the cleric who was Lilly's brother-in-law, was not the plaintiff, but the theft may have occurred at Trefach where Laugharne was said to have lived. The prosecutor was Thomas Roch of St David's, but Lilly escaped from Haverfordwest gaol where he was awaiting transportation, to join up with William Owen some time after. (*NLW, Great Sessions minute book 15/53, 160*). Also in March 1745, at Cardigan Great Sessions, James Moss was committed for felony and it was ordered that he be 'burnt in the hand', i.e. branded with the letter 'T'. One wonders if this was the same 'John Moss' who had been prosecuted on 13 January 1744 OS (i.e. 1745) for the robbery of wearing apparel at Gwnnws (Llanwnnws, 6 miles north of Tregaron, and 12 miles south-east of Aberystwyth).

Governor Lindesay was not at all pleased to see William's return to Man, and the *James and Bridget* was still impounded.

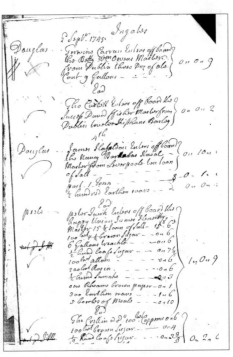

Douglas Ingates 2 September 1745

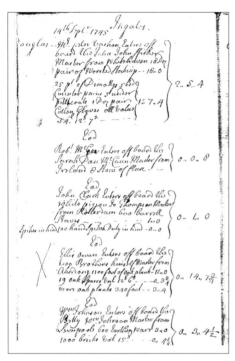

Douglas Ingates 14 September 1745

William's creditors were circling, but he says he went smuggling in South Wales. Owen also claims that he was asked to fight for the Stuart rebels, and the Pretender, 'Bonnie Prince Charlie' landed in Scotland on 23 July 1745, was in Edinburgh by 17 September, and upon 8 November marched into England with no Hanoverian opposition. Carlisle surrendered to the Scots on 26 December 1745, but Charles Stuart was defeated at Culloden upon 16 April 1746, ending all hopes of the 31-year-old Germanic royal dynasty being overthrown.

In the summer of 1745 William sailed a 'pacquet' (packet boat) carrying mail, passengers and freight between Dublin and Man. This appears to have begun upon 2 May and continued until 2 July 1745. The latter date is confirmed by the *Dublin Journal*, and Owen halted sailing the Douglas Packet crossings after two months 'according to his agreement'. He may well have been involved in other trade, as upon 22 June 1745, the ingates record at Douglas reads 'Wm Owen Enters off Board the *Two* [this may be Three] *Brothers* himself Master from

Cardigan 26 barrels of Barley 17s 4d.' On the same day the next entries are 'Ellis Owen 29 bowles of wheat 9s 8d' (presumably William's relative) and John McMarron with 22 bowles Rys 1s 4d.' The following entry is 'Dav Evans Enters off board the *Two Brothers* himself Master from Cardigan' with a cargo of barley, rice, wheat and oats upon which he paid £1 6s 9d. (These may possibly be different boats – Owen's ship's name is indistinct, but does not read like 'Two'. Hopefully there were not two William Owens operating as ship's masters at this time.)

On 2 September 1745 we read in the Douglas ingates records: 'Torwins? Carran Enters off board the *Betty*' with 'Wm Owens Master from Dublin' paying just 9 pence duty upon 'three doz of ale Cont 9 Gallons. Carran could well be William Carron (Carroun), or one of his relatives. At Douglas, upon 14 September 1745, 'Ellis Owen (Owen's cousin) Enters off board the *Two Brothers* himself Master from Aberdovey,' carrying '1,100 foot of oak plank 11s 0d; 19 oak spars val 12s 6d – 3 ¾d; more oak planks 340 foot 3s 4d': with 14s 7¾d in duty to pay.

However, in September 1745 Owen was to sail from Dublin for South Wales, smuggling with a relative, probably Ellis Owen, but could not go, because of an impending law suit. (The 'confession' is very tangled at this stage, and open to several interpretations). The court case involved ownership of the *James and Bridget*, and there were claims and counter-claims. Owen had many creditors, with Edward Stockley petitioning for the return of his share in the impounded *James and Bridget*. William knew that failure to attend the hearing on 7 November could give rise to his expulsion from the relative safety of Man. The smuggling expedition set out on 2 November, and on 3 November was wrecked, with the loss of all hands, including William's wife. He learned of the loss somewhere between Llanbadarn and Aberdovey when he sailed to Wales in November, and it was confirmed two months later in

Pembrokeshire. He had lost cargo worth £160, and after staying stayed with friends in Cardigan, in March 1746 returned to Dublin, becoming a ship's mate.

In 1745 there was a report to the Collector of Customs at Milford Haven: 'Mr Owen having applied to us by his memorial of 28th ultimo relating to a cask of brandy taken up at sea and seized by Thomas Lloyd officer at Dale, Inclosed we send you a copy of the said memorial and you are to examine into the allegation therein contained in a report a true state of the case to us with your opinion.' (*CUST75/5f134*). Enclosed was a memorial dated 21 October 1745: 'Honourable Sirs, Having received information on oath that Mr Thomas Lloyd one of your officers at Dale in the Port of Milford has taken up at sea a cask of brandy which belongs to me as vice admiral however he has refused to deliver it and says he can't do it without your orders & has sent it to the Custom house, on which account I trouble you with this to claim the brandy and to desire it may be delivered up to me, as my right to it can't be doubted, if it

Dale, where the customs officer was accused by Owen in October 1745

should be necessary to give security for the duty if any person in the time limited should claim it (which is impossible) I am ready to do it. William Owen.'

After two voyages, one of which featured the altercation with Lloyd, in July 1746 William served as master of a 20-gun privateer, the *Admiral Blake* from Liverpool. Liverpool had 188 ships in 1744, of which just 4 were privateers: *Terrible*, carrying 22 guns and 180 men, mentioned above, upon which William says he served in 1736; Captain James Powell's Norfolk-built 250-ton *Old Noll*, with the same guns and men; Captain Dugdale's 70-ton *Thurloe*, a Rhode Island-built snow with 12 guns and 100 men; and Captain Edmondson's *Admiral Blake*, of unknown capacity. To put privateering into perspective, in 1753 Liverpool had 53 slave ships sailing on the 'Triangular Trade', but the life expectancy of slaver crews, many impressed men (not only the Royal Navy forcibly 'pressed' men into service), was around 18 months, owing to the 'bloody flux', malaria, yellow fever and other diseases to which slaves had more resistance.

William Owen sailed into Cobh in the *Admiral Blake* in January 1747 after a poor voyage. (She previously had left Liverpool in April 1746 and returned in May without taking a prize. Her next voyage was far more successful, with three French prizes being sailed into Lisbon in November 1747). Many of her crew had died of disease off the Barbary Coast and William was extremely ill. (The 'Berber Coast' now comprises the coastlines of Morocco, Algeria, Tunisia and Libya). Not quite recovered, he moved to Dublin, but relapsed and became impoverished. He returned to Cardigan to recuperate, and then in South Wales fell in with the St Dogmael's fencing master, James Lilly. They took up burglary and highway robbery. William had brought an action of trespass against Lilly in 1742 concerning work done by him for Lilly, freighting goods in 1740.

The dispute was sent to arbitration but the result is not known (*NLW, Great Sessions 18/272/m.1; Great Sessions 14/53, 160*).

According to *Penny London Post* (10 April 1747), William Owen and Lilly burgled the house of John Thomas of Nevern in April 1747, stealing twenty guineas and shooting a servant. Lilly, not Owen, was called a 'notorious smuggler'. This may have been a substantial place, as the current value of the theft is over £3,000. There seems to have been little local reporting of the crime, but the *General Advertiser* of 10 April 1747 reported: 'Cardigan April 2. A burglary was committed in this neighbourhood in the Night time, on Sunday the 29th ult. by two Villains masked, who broke open the Dwelling House of one John Thomas, a Farmer, and stole thence Twenty Guineas, but one of the Men Servants being awake and hearing a Noise and got out of Bed, when one of the Villains shot him in the Face, and there are but small Hopes of his Recovery. A Hue and Cry being raised, Search was made, and Letters sent to all the Parts, but no Tidings could be had of the Villains. But on Sunday Morning early, they were seen passing through this Town, and being observed which way they steered, Pursuit was made, and our Post Boy being foremost among the Pursuers, one of them called James Lilly, a Drawing Master, shot at and killed his horse and the other Villain, called William Owen, Mariner, shot at and killed him upon the spot; notwithstanding which they next continued their Pursuit, and came in View of them, but Owen, for what Reason is not known, in the upper parts of Carmarthenshire, shot his Comrade Lilly, and on the close of night was forced to yield and surrender himself Prisoner.*

Both the villains were well armed with several large Horse Pistols, and well stocked with Ammunition. NB The said Lilly was last Sessions tried for Burglary, and sentence of Transportation passed upon him, but he broke gaol and fled to

Ireland. Owen was tried two Years since at Hereford, for shooting the Customs House Officer, and his Assistant.** Both of them were very notorious Villains and Smugglers, and each of them had several wives now living. *He is brought to Carmarthen castle where he is confined a close prisoner.' **in this port and harbour.'

The Gloucester Journal (14 April 1747) also printed a report from Cardigan, dated 2 April: 'A burglary took place in the neighbourhood on Sunday night 29 March by two villains who broke into the dwelling house of John Thomas, a farmer, and stole 20 guineas: a manservant who woke and went to look was shot in the face with small hope of recovery. A Hue and Cry was raised and on Tuesday the two men were seen in the town and chased. Among the followers was the post boy whose horse was shot and killed by James Lilley [sic], a dancing master, one of the villains. The boy was shot and killed by William Owen. The two villains then crossed into Carmarthenshire where that night William Owen shot and killed James Lilley. He was forced to yield and taken to Carmarthen to stand trial. Executed 2 May 1747.'

Thus a few days after the Nevern robbery, the pair were seen in Cardigan, and a 'hue and cry' gave pursuit. (By law, anyone who witnessed a crime had to effect a hue and cry, and keep it up against the fleeing criminal from town to town, and from county to county, until the felon was apprehended and delivered to the sheriff. All able-bodied men, upon hearing the shouts of hue and cry, had to assist in the pursuit of the criminal. It was stated that 'the whole hundred ... shall be answerable' for any theft or robbery, i.e. a collective punishment. Those who raised a hue and cry falsely were themselves guilty of a crime.) Lilly shot the horse of the leading chaser in the hue and cry, then Owen shot its rider, the Cardigan 'post boy' Evan George. This explains why Owen stated, that after his arrest he was gaoled 'on suspicion of killing the Cardigan post, but not charged then with the killing of Lilly'. Evan George's widow was awarded 20 shillings, and 6 members of the hue and cry were given 40 shillings between them by the Cardiganshire Quarter Session, 'for the future encouragement of persons pursuing such notorious malefactors' (*Ceredigion Archives, Easter Sessions* 1747).

The pair were seen passing through Llangeler, and stopped for refreshments at John Thomas's inn where they were spotted again. According to Arwyn Williams of Penlan Farm, Llanfihangel-ar-Arth, this was at Pentrecwrt, and may have been the Black Lion in that village. An alternative suggestion is the Porth, near Llandysul's church. The Thomases owned the inn in the early 19th century, so they may have had it a few decades earlier. Owen shot Lilly on the old road from Llanfihangel to Mynydd Llanllwni, at a field still called Cae Lilly. Owen was then taken on Llanllwni Mountain, not being able to escape the hue and cry. It seems that William Owen, who was on foot and ill, shot Lilly, so that he could take his horse and escape, but he was captured on 6 April. A coroner's inquest brought in a verdict of murder. He was indicted and tried at Carmarthen on 17 April 1747 and again defended himself, saying he was innocent of Lilly's killing. Aged perhaps thirty, he was convicted and hung in Carmarthen on 2 May 1747. After his confession, William Owen gives us a brief explanation of his 'Character and Behaviour', proudly describing all his virtues but admitting to lust and occasional pride. He omits previous knowledge of Lilly, his conviction for manslaughter at Hereford, and the hue and cry set up after the Nevern burglary in which he badly wounded or killed a servant, and his killing of Evan George and James Lilly to escape the chase.

In April 1747, we see 'The King against Owen for Murder. Upon motion of Mr Nares ordered that the Horse taken upon the Defendant is to be surrendered with its two pistols to be delivered to the Attorney-General who is steward of the Manor where he was taken.' The attorney-general for South Wales (the counties of Cardigan, Carmarthen, and Pembroke), was John Lloyd, barrister at law, who succeeded his father Walter as attorney-general. The Lloyds owned the great estate of Voelallt (Foelallt), Llanddewi Brefi, Ceredigion, and Walter had married the heiress of Daniel Evans of the nearby estate of Peterwell, Lampeter. He was mayor of Cardigan five times, and M.P. for Cardiganshire, 1734-42. Walter's eldest surviving son John was M.P. for Cardiganshire from 1747 until his death in 1755. Childless, he was succeeded by his brother, the notorious Herbert Lloyd of Peterwell.

We see that on 15 Apr 1748 William Corrin (quite possibly William's crew member William Carron, married Mary Kelly at Lonan, Isle of Man. It is tempting to think that this was William Owen's widow. Lonan parish is in the Sheading of Garff, as was Onchan, where William Owen sheltered with his 'Manx wife'.

In his book *Two Dragons*, Howard Marks tells of his life as 'one of the most sophisticated drug barons of all time'. He describes how a prison conversation with a murderer called Tee Bone, persuaded him to look into his family history. Marks said 'shortly after my father's death in October 1996, and one month after the publication of Mr Nice [his autobiography] I decided to search the attic... I knew so little about my ancestry but now, for the first time in my life, I wanted to learn more. He discovered a distant relative, William Owen, known as The Terrible, a famous Welsh smuggler whose chronicle of scams, acquittals and debauchery would put any modern-day smuggler or playboy to shame'.

Footnote 1: A note upon Cae Lilly

The Rev. William Nantlais Williams of Pencader (1874-1959), a few miles from Cae Lilly wrote of the spirit of John Lilly haunting the fields, and being known as 'Lili Wen' (white lily). 'Nantlais' was from Gwyddgrug in the parish of Llanfihangel-ar-Arth, and wrote that a young man of the area decided to challenge the spirit, which he had frequently seen. Accordingly he ventured up Alltwalis hill, carrying an axe to seek the ghost. (Gwyddgrug, Alltwalis, New Inn, Dolgran and Pencader are all in the parish of Llanfihangel-ar-Arth). Arwyn Williams has farmed Penlan, between Llanfihangel-ar-Arth and Llandysul, Carmarthenshire, for over fifty years. He recalls a previous occupant, Martha Davies recounting that during the war, when lights at nights were forbidden, that she and local people would avoid walking the road between the villages, as the then road passed Cae Lilly, the field haunted by James Lilly. Mr Williams

Arwyn Williams of Penlan Farm, standing in Cae Lilly,
where Owen shot James Lilly

recounts that in tradition Owen and Lilly were spotted eating at Pentrecwrt before Lilly was shot, and that Owen was captured upon Llanllwni Mountain.

In *The Transactions of the Carmarthenshire Antiquarian Society and Field Club* (XXV 1934), we read that on 26 April 1752 Griffith Philipps wrote to his son George: 'There are this day to be hang's at Carmarthen two men for housebreaking, which I suppose will bring all ye country peoples together, it being a very common thing here to get 'em hanged by pairs'. The editor of the *Cwmgwili Manuscripts* added a footnote: 'Who these two people were I know not, but public hangings in Carmarthen were then terribly frequent. In 1747 Captain Owens, a noted smuggler, was executed for killing one Lilley, a dancing master who, to save himself from transportation broke out of Haverford prison.' J. Frederick Jones, the author of the article *Cae Lilley: Llanfihangel Ioreth*, adds information given by his friend John Jones, of Bancyffordd, Llandysul: 'When I was a boy I had this story from the old people – A man named Lili or Lilley had killed a man in the lower part of Pembrokeshire (Godre Sir Benfro). He escaped along the mountains as far as the parish of Llanfihangel-Ioreth. He was shot on the mountain, and his body was taken to the nearest cross roads, where, according to the custom of the time, he was buried.

The field adjoining the crossroads is called "Cae Lilley" to this day. The cross-roads are mid-way between Llandyssul Bridge and Llanfihangel-Ioreth parish church, on the Llandyssul-Lampeter road, and are known as "Penlan Old Cross-Roads." The field "Cae Lilly" is close to the cross-roads, and forms part of Penlan farm.' The old Penlan crossroads are now in the field adjoining Cae Lilly, as new roads have replaced the old tracks. The road from Llandysul to Carmarthen on the east side of the Teifi passed through Maesycrugiau, joining the stage coach road from Carmarthen to Lampeter. Maesycrugiau was then known as Llanllwni, where the church of St Llwni, or Llonio, and the adjacent site of its castle, rise above the Teifi there. When the new road ran parallel inland in the early nineteenth century, the spread of houses along it became known as Llanllwni and Llanllwni was renamed Maesycrugiau after the nearby manor with its two burial mounds (*crugiau*). The line of the old road on Penland Farm can be made out by field boundaries. We must also note that *mynydd*, mountain, also signifies a large hill, so nearby Mynydd Llanllwni and Mynydd Llanybydder are not, in reality, mountains.

J. Frederick Jones goes on to write that John Jones 'suggests that Lilley, the dancing master, sentenced to transportation, who escaped from Haverfordwest prison, and was subsequently shot by Captain Owens, and Lilli or Lilley, the murderer, from "Godre Sir Benfro", who was killed and buried at "Penlan Old Cross-roads," in the parish of Llanfihangel-Ioreth are one and the same man.' On a separate note, the Celtic church site Mihangel (Michael) is certainly a Norman rededication of a 6th-century Welsh saint, and one would posit Iorwerth or Iorath as its original dedication. 'Ar arth' seems to be a corruption of Iorath, and there is no named stream near the church, which is above the Teifi. There was a holy well, Ffynnon Yeroth in Llanarthne, Carmarthenshire noted in 1625 parish deeds, and this could well be the same person. The rededication of churches across Wales helped destroy Welsh history, as virtually all of its documents and holy sites were burnt or destroyed during over a millennium of invasions and conflict. The EU diktat of compulsory numbering of fields has led to names being lost, many of which are associated with saints or their holy wells.

Fortunately most Welsh-speaking farmers prefer the ancient names of their fields. Cae Lilly is the only recent name upon Arwyn Williams' farm at Penlan, indicating the veracity of his death there a quarter of a millennium ago. In Arwyn's fields, *coch*, mutated to *goch*, indicated red oak leaves covering the field in Autumn. His other field names are cae pistyll (well field), cae'r odyn (kiln field), cae rhiw (slope field), cae ffynnon (spring field), cae'r banc (bank field), cae'r ardd (garden field), (also cae bach yr ardd), fron dan penrhiw (brow under the top slope), fron newydd (new brow), pen yr allt goch (red head of the hill), ddol wair (cut hay meadow), blaentir (front ground), cae pant (field in the hollow), cae plwmp (straight field), cae mawr (great field), cae cnwc (hillock field), cae typorth (gatehouse field), cae bola haul (sun bathed field), fron dan y cwarai (brow beneath the quarry), and ddol goch (red meadow). The adjacent farm name of Bribwll, and cae Bribwll indicates to some experts that there was a wolf-pit there, where a carcass would be placed to attract wolves (extinct in Wales in the early medieval period), who could not then escape. Bribwll is the oral form of bleiddbwll, where a covering of branches and twigs disguised the pit. In Cae Lilly was found in 1958 a Bronze Age urn from around 1600 BCE, and there were three prehistoric ditches on the farm. David Evans of Penlan led Rebecca Rioters, and was prosecuted for an attack on the nearby toll-house, when c.70 men disguised as women destroyed the tollgate in June 1843. A 16 December 1842 anonymous letter from one of the rioters ('Becca and her children') threatened the gate at nearby 'Llanengel', which gives further corroboration of Lily's death near Llanfihangel. (*National Archives HO 45/265 fn.1*). In fact, two gates were destroyed, one in Pencader and then the one at 'Lanfihangel-Yeroth', with the special constables dedicated with guarding them being threatened at gunpoint. One was ordered to help demolishing the gate, and to return the next day to take away the gateposts.

George Eyre Evans transcribed the Rice letters for the

Carmarthenshire Antiquarian Society, and writes: 'A Rebecca leader was David Evans, who at the Summer Assizes, opened before Sir Robert Monsy Rolfe, at Carmarthen on 13 July, 1844, was tried for being concerned in pulling down and destroying Llanfihangel-ar-Arth Gate on 19 June 1843, and found "guilty of being in the company, but not guilty of demolishing." On Wednesday, 17 July, he was again tried, this time for destroying Gwarallt Gate [on 10 July near Llanllwni – it was said that 200 'daughters' were involved]. 'The jury, having been locked up all night not agreeing, the Judge ordered the prisoner to be discharged, but told him that he might be called again at the next or any Assizes to be tried for the same offence before another jury.' The 4th Lord Dynevor, responsible for policing Carmarthenshire, took matters so seriously he ordered a detachment of Metropolitan Police into Carmarthenshire from London, a response which would be repeated almost 150 years later during the 1984/85 Miners' Strike. From November 1842 to late 1843, over 250 tollgates were destroyed in west Wales, most of them several times, with the houses that went with them usually suffering the same fate. Lord Dynevor wrote of David Evans' discharge: 'I am sorry to have missed seeing you at Carmarthen, though we had but little business. I am sorry to say our Petty Jury disgraced themselves most terribly in acquitting a Rebecca leader, in spite of his own acknowledgment of having been present at the time a Toll-house was destroyed, on which occasion two witnesses swore he was actively engaged. He said "I did no more than the others" who, however, pulled the house down amongst them.'

David Evans was the local leader of the rioters, and I cannot find any record of his being fined, imprisoned or transported for the three criminal acts. Born around 1796, the Penlan farmer was said to be 48 when tried, and had four children. He could 'read and write imperfectly', had a fair complexion and was an imposing 5ft 11 ½ inches in height. More upon David Evans is contained in Chapter 8. There was an incredible unwillingness to inform upon the rioters or to convict them, and this additional information is included because just one field on Penlan Farm saw a nearby wolf-pit, an important Bronze Age burial, pre-Christian entrenchments, a former important cross-roads, the killing of a highwayman, the escape of a smuggler and murderer, and a hero of the Rebecca Riots. This is Wales – it has unknown and ignored history across the nation.

Footnote 2: John Davies, Minister

The final page of Owen's confession formally certifies that that the whole manuscript is 'genuine and authentic', having been 'examined' by Owen himself; signed by Owen on 24 April 1747, and witnessed by John Davies, minister of St. Mary's, Carmarthen. Owen was captured upon 6 April, and was kept in Carmarthen Castle Gaol until his trial in Carmarthen on 16 April. It therefore must have been written from 17 April until his execution upon 2 May, a period of about two weeks. In 1743 Rev. John Davies became the rector of the premier church in Cardigan, St Mary's until at least August 1777. It seems that he was the divine who ministered to William Owen during his imprisonment in Carmarthen Gaol in 1747, as there is no sign of a Carmarthen minister of that name, and he will have known of Owen, as would have all of Cardigan's inhabitants. John Davies may well have re-written the confession, ensuring that its readers realise that all crimes are punished. This didactic purpose appears, vanishes and resurfaces throughout the remarkably humourless account, with William Owen being seemingly unconcerned about killing unarmed men, visiting brothels and siring illegitimate children but admiring good manners, virginity and hating over-consumption of alcohol, especially in women. His rebellion against long-suffering and generous parents, unwise marriage(s), desertion, lying, breaking of indentures and pretences to a higher station in life as a 'gentleman' all indicate a road to perdition and could well have been intensified by John Davies.

As a sign of Owen's times, in 1743 St. Mary's Church poor-box was robbed. On 14th August 1745 work was proposed to complete the tower. Glen Johnson, 'the Teifi Estuary Man' (*glen-johnson.co.uk*), tells us that the 'upper part of the church tower was finally completed in 1748. A plaque was unveiled that year commemorating all of the benefactors. The Vicar that year was Rev. William Powell.' St Mary's Church is on the site of a 12th Century Benedictine Priory, and during the 13th century the Church found fame by being a site of pilgrimage as the shrine of 'Our Lady of the Taper'. However, in 1537, the abolition of pilgrimages deprived a profitable income from this Shrine of Our Lady of Cardigan.

On 16 March 1538, Thomas Barlow, the detested Bishop of St. David's, visited what he called the 'shamefull detestacion called Our Ladyes taper of Cardigan'. He interrogated the Vicar of St. Mary's and Prior of Cardigan about the shrine. It consisted of a statue of the Virgin Mary with the Holy Child, which had once held a taper in her hand. Barlow's concern was with the taper, rather that the statue itself, as this had long been venerated as a relic. He also questioned the Vicar, Morgan Meredith, and Barlow dismissed the taper as 'a pece of olde rottene tymber.' The taper was sent to Thomas Cromwell and the statue was burned in Chelsea, soon afterwards. Both the Prior and the Vicar were ordered to preach the folly of idolatry worship. A shrine still exists at St Mary's, although it is not the original.

Footnote 3 – The Mathias Connection

The existing manuscript is a copy of the 1747 original, written by Daniel G. Matthias, who has signed inside the front cover, with a date of January 1811. The Matthias family will have been well acquainted with both William Owen, and the Rev. John Davies at St Mary's Church. Isaac Matthias was Cardigan's Surveyor of Customs, who died aged 46 on 25 December 1807, and was buried on 27 December at St Mary`s Church, Cardigan. Isaac Matthias may have died of Yellow Fever. It was generally called distemper at this time, spread on slave trade ships and thus often attacked ports. In the *Staffordshire Advertiser* (23 January 1808) we read: 'It is much to our concern that a dreadful distemper rages in & about the town of Cardigan South Wales. Whole families have been cut off & many houses bereaved of their tenants. Among the recent deaths are Mrs Davies wife of Mr H Davies Shopkeeper. Mr George Davies of the White Hart Inn. Mr Isaac Matthias one of the Custom House Officers. Mrs Ferrier wife of John Ferrier Esq of the Cardigan Militia. Mr Rowland Watkins many years a respectable Innkeeper at Eglwyswrw near Cardigan. Griffith Edwards many years a noted performer on the Violin in Cardigan. Mrs Jones wife of David Jones a respectable farmer at Ffynnon – Criphill near Cardigan.'

Isaac Matthias may have well have left the Owen ms. to his son, our signatory Daniel Gwynne Matthias, and is quite possibly related to Sir Henry Matthias of Fern Hill, Pembrokeshire. Sir Henry was the Prothonotary of the Carmarthen circuit from 1783 until the Court of Great Sessions was abolished in 1830, and may have held the original manuscript. Isaac's son Daniel Gwynne Matthias was also an Officer of Customs, as was Daniel's own son Isaac Rice Matthias. Isaac Rice Matthias worked at Cardiff Docks as an Officer of Customs, dying of Cholera (another epidemic in ports of the time) in 1854. There was a family variously spelt Matthias and Mathias living in Nevern parish in William Owen's time, and again it may have passed into their hands by this route.

Footnote 4 – William Owen's Time Line

If researchers wish to 'fill in the gaps' in Owen's erratic life, the following may help. I add Lilly as his life (and death) is interlinked with that of William Owen.

[James Lilly, dancing master, fencing master and teacher of drawing born 1695];

Owen born c.1717;

Shipped on a Bristol trader from Haverfordwest;

Returned to farm, then shipped on a Bideford vessel;

15 February 1735 Owen married Anne Nicholas at Cardigan;

9 November 1735, daughter Ann born;

[30 November 1735 James Lilly married again, to Anne Laugharne of Llanreithan];

Returned to farm, father bought him a vessel c.1735 – sailed to Isle of Man;

Sailed as 2nd mate on the *Joy* from Bristol to Barbados c. May 1736;

Deserted in 1736 and joined the privateer *Terrible* as a mate in Barbados, organized defence against Spanish off Venezuela;

In 'fighting command' of *Mayflower*, Bay of Honduras. Attacked by Spanish coastguards;

Captained *Fly* to Salamanca (Colombia) attacked by coastguards, Antigua, Martinique, Barbados;

Probably impressed on *HMS Oxford* around February 1737 when it was in Barbados (or taken at sea after chase);

30 August 1737 Owen's son William is baptised at Cardigan;

After 20 months at sea, c. January 1738, receives letter that he has a son;

Returned home after 42 months at sea, c. November 1739, most spent on *Oxford*;

[1739 James and Anne Lilly receive £491 12s 6d from will];

His father gave him money in 'Autumn' (probably 1739) to buy a vessel, the *Dispatch* in Swansea;

1740 in Dublin, embargo blocked his trade of James Lilly's cargo; sold *Dispatch*, bought *Blessing* and refitted her;

[1 July 1740 court case brought by Owen against Lilly for non-payment of £40];

1st March 1741, *Blessing* ransacked by mob in Cardigan/St Dogmael's, Owen shot their leader;

31 July 1741, Bristol port records that Owen was the master of the *Blessing* of Cardigan, trading there;

March 1742 the Court of Great Sessions records that James Lilly of Tregaron owed Owen £40;

14 June 1742, Thomas Johnes of Abermâd's tenants attacked Thomas Parry's house, and Owen says he attacked Johnes' mansion in retaliation;

19 February 1743 Owen took a cargo as Master of the *Blessing* from Waterford to Douglas, Man;

Smuggling from Waterford to St Bride's Bay, rebuilt *Blessing* and renamed her *Prince Charles*;

Prince Charles sailed to Waterford, Man (here he may have met/married Mary Kelly in January 1743), Liverpool (by foot), Milnthorpe, Man, Whitehaven, Workington, and she was boarded by Customs in February 1743;

1st March 1743 Owen battled the Customs cruiser *Sincerity*, and sailed to Man on 2 March – he possibly 'married' Mary Kelly around this time;

8 June 1743 the Collector of Whitehaven records that Owen is thought of as a pirate, and is operating under the alias Joshua Lewis, having obstructed a Customs sloop;

10 June 1743 Owen sails the *Molly* and *Betty* as master from Liverpool into Douglas;

Sailed to South Wales, Fishguard, St Bride's, Haverfordwest (on foot) and Cardigan, fought Irish smugglers;

Sailed into Cardigan to pay off his 'dead drunk' wife's debts and renounced her;

Sailed to Man, South Wales, Laugharne, Carmarthen, Haverfordwest, Man;

Sailed to Grange-over-Sands, Kendal (on foot);

Smuggling into Westmorland, the *Prince Charles* is seized in his absence at Kendal. Penniless, he heads to Cardigan to raffle a cow, and his new 'wife' goes from Liverpool to Man.

On 26 November 1743 there is an order for William Owen of Douglas to keep the peace towards James Kinsale;

From Man he sailed for Liverpool with tea; and on next voyage on a Manx boat to Duddon, Cumberland as pilot;

From Man he sailed to Barmouth, selling goods in Chester;

On 4 February 1744, in Conwy he part-purchased the *James and Bridget* from Edward Pugh of Penryn Old Hall;

12 March 1744 sailed into Cardigan;

4 April 1744 killed two customs officers and two Spaniards at Cardigan, and fled to Man;

28 April James Moss in Man made a deposition of Owen's killings at Cardigan;

Owen's ship was taken and Governor Lindesay wrote on 30 April to Lord Atholl that Owen had escaped with wife to Peel and then Ireland;

End of April, Owen arrived on an Irish oyster boat at Strangford Lough, then Downpatrick;

1 May 1744, Christian's inn at Onchan was searched for Owen;

11 May 1744 *London Gazette* reports Owen's killing of James Phillips and William Hughes at Cardigan;

Owen and wife moved to Lurgan at the end of May 1744;

June 1744, Lewis and Carron of his crew were arrested in Man and tried to enlist in the Navy to avoid imprisonment;

August Callow of his crew arrested in Liverpool;

[17 August 1744 a case against James Lilly at Carmarthen];

From Dublin Owen made for Wales, then for Man arriving at Christian's inn on 29 August, narrowly escaped from

Christian's inn on 5 September 1744;

Ambushed on 7 September and taken to Castle Rushen;

12 October, Owen and his crew are taken on the *Sincerity* to Cardigan Bay, but fear to land and head for Liverpool;

Owen tried for murder at Hereford 16 March 1745, verdict of manslaughter, returned to Douglas, Man, smuggled to South Wales and returned to Man;

March 1745, Lilly found guilty of theft and sentenced to 7 years transportation but escaped from Haverfordwest gaol and took to robbery;

2 May – 2 July 1745 Owen went 'legitimate' on the Dublin packet trade to Man and back;

22 June 1745 Owen on the *Two (or Three) Brothers* from Cardigan took goods to Douglas;

2 September 1745 Owen sails as Master on the *Betty* from Dublin;

September 1745 Owen involved in lawsuit, which prevented him travelling with wife, who drowned on 2 October;

21 October 1745, Owen reports the Dale Customs Collector for illegally confiscating a barrel of brandy;

Travelled between Liverpool, Llanbadarn and Pembroke, discovered his wife was dead in March 1746, began an affair in Dublin;

From March 1746 made two voyages as master;

July 1746, master of privateer *Admiral Blake*, sailing from Cobh to Barbary Coast, convalescing in Dublin and returning January 1747, gravely ill to Liverpool;

Returned to South Wales. Fell in with James Lilly, robbed a house in Nevern on 29 March 1747, shooting a servant in the face;

Spotted in Cardigan, chased by Hue and Cry, and Lilly shot the leading pursuer's horse. Owen then shot its rider, Evan George, before shooting Lilly to take his horse;

6 April Owen was captured, sentenced to death on 17 April, hung at Carmarthen on 2 May.

Chapter 5

A Note on Carmarthen Executions

From 1746, anyone found guilty of injuring or killing a Revenue man would be sentenced to death, and those guilty of smuggling had a choice of joining the Royal Navy, going to prison or paying a fine.

From the sixteenth to the eighteenth centuries, Carmarthen was the most highly populated borough in Wales, described by William Camden as 'the chief citie of the country'. Carmarthen had prospered, being described as 'the ffarest Towne in all South Wales, and of most Scivillytie' in 1548, the year after William Owen's execution. It was the most populous town in Wales before the Industrial Revolution, but in 1750, Carmarthen still only had 500 houses.

Carmarthen Circuit Session executions 1739-1798

Before the end of the 18th century there were more than 150 offences for which death was the specified penalty. From 1752 – 1836 hanging was carried out on the second day following sentencing unless it was a Sunday (in which case the execution took place on Monday). In some cases, the judge could respite the death sentence, while the condemned sought a reprieve. Sometimes, the gallows were ordered to be built on the spot where the crime had been committed, so erecting the gallows could delay proceedings. The body was usually dissected before burial, and put on public display, or in the worst cases hung in chains (gibbetted). Hangings were nearly always carried out in public. In Carmarthen, Babel Hill in Pensarn was the place for county executions before 1818, on the site where Babell Chapel now stands, and those of town criminals on the Royal Oak

Common, in Johnstown. By the end of the 18th century, it became clear that the mile-long walk from Carmarthen Gaol to the gallows led to crowd disturbances, and the condemned suffered additional stress. Thus, after 1818, all condemned persons (including forgers) were executed on a new public gallows, on a platform raised inside and above the Carmarthen County Gaol wall, facing Spilman Street.

The last man to suffer the 'death walk' to Pensarn was Rees Thomas Rees in April 1817, for the 'murder' of his sweetheart. She had swallowed a concoction which he had bought, to attempt an abortion of their child. Brought from gaol, Rees was placed in a chaise and carried through 10,000 spectators. As he ascended the gallows at Pensarn, ministers started praying and the crowds joined in. The last public execution at Carmarthen Gaol was that of David Evans in 1829, and the crowd who saw it stretched up as far as the Ivy Bush. They also had a free view of the body afterwards.

It almost 60 years (1888) before Carmarthen held another execution, by then was which time it was no longer a public spectacle. We see that only 21 hangings were ordered on the Carmarthen circuit between 1739 and 1798, just one every three years, at a time when the death penalty was commonly imposed for theft and burglary.

22 May 1739 – a man named Edwards, from Llandefeilog was said to be hanged at Pensarn for pilfering, but there seems to be no record.

23 May 1739 – Elinor Williams, alias Hadley, a single woman was tried – 'on 2 March 1739 in the parish of St Peter in the town and county of Carmarthen gave birth to a male child which she assaulted violently so that the child instantly died.' The inquest on the child's body stated that there were marks of violence on the right side of the head. She was convicted of the murder of her child, and hung 26 May. A servant at Job's Well, she was

hanged on the 'Common below Royal Oak Gate'. Buried near Carmarthen railway station, her body is reported have been placed in the gibbet before burial.

23 May 1739 – two young lads, David Rees and Evan Lloyd were said to be prosecuted and sentenced to hanging for stealing cider from Mr Evan Thomas, landlord of the Greyhound Inn, Carmarthen. They were were ordered to be executed on 4 August but reprieved. They may have been transported to the colonies.

1742 According to the *executionwales.blogspot.co.uk* in this year a 'girl aged just 8 years old, was tried at Carmarthen Assizes. She had been charged with the murder of her brother and sister, ages 6 & 4 respectively. It appeared the children were frightened by stories making the rounds about the cruelty inflicted by the Spaniards and the expected Spanish invasion. During the night, a violent thunderstorm erupted and the children believed it was the invading Spaniards. The young children begged their sister to kill them. She carried out the killings with a blade used to trim hedging. She then attempted to use the blade on herself. Records show this child was acquitted at her trial.'

6 April 1745 – Robert Lewis Richard was convicted of the murder of Edward Owen, and hung 24 April.

6 April 1745 – David Evan was convicted of burglary – hung 24 April.

11 April 1747 – Capt. William Owen was convicted of the murder of James Lilley [sic] – hung at Pensarn Hill, Carmarthen 2 May.

1750, according to the blogspot *executionwales* saw 'the hanging of Joseph Jenkins, "a noted swearer was committed to the town gaol for the murder of his wife."' Once convicted, he was hanged on the common near the Royal Oak Gate. St Peter's Register records the murder as '1750 December 11th'.

3 April 1751 – Joseph Jenkins convicted of murder of wife – hung 17 April.

7 April 1752 John Delahay and James Williams convicted of burglary – hung 25 April (Part of a 1752 letter from Griffith Philips of Cwmgwili to his son George in London reads: 'there are this day to be hang'd at Carmarthen two men for house breaking, which I suppose will draw al ye country peoples together, it being a very uncommon thing here to get em hang'd in pairs.')

15 April 1767 – Phillip Phillip convicted of murder of Elizabeth James – hung in chains at Newcastle Emlyn, 22 April.

7 September 1767 – Edward Higgins convicted of burglary – hung at Pensarn 7 November.

30 August 1773 – William Thomas convicted of horse theft – hung at Pensarn 18 September. [see note following this list of executions]

Autumn 1774 – John Thomas convicted of Horse theft – hung 10 September.

25 August 1783 – Griffith Rowland convicted of murder of David John – hung 30 August.

24 March 1784 – Thomas John convicted of murder of daughter – hung 31 March.

28 August 1786 – Edward Rees convicted of cattle theft – hung 23 September.

4 April 1787 – William Griffiths convicted of burglary – hung 21 April.

2 August 1788 – William Emmanuel convicted of murder of Margaret David – hung 9 August, and afterwards hung in chains on Pembrey Common. (Richard Jones of Carmarthen contradicts this single record, writing in 1788 to John George Philipps M.P, 'we had three persons condemned, two for horse stealing and one for stealing goods and breaking into a house in the day time; this last was the hangman in the gaol, a person

not 20 years of age, who had been tried at our bar three times; not half an hour after he received sentence he hung himself in the gaol.')

1788 – *executionwales* blogspot records that this year 'kept the hangman busy at Pensarn with several executions. One of these was Will Mani, for murdering a woman on Pembrey Mountain. The cuff from his coat was found in his victim's hand and was identified by a tailor and convicted Mani. He was hanged then gibbeted on the hill at Pensarn. Gutto (Grifeith) Rowley was charged with murdering a tithe collector. He escaped to Bristol and worked in a sugar warehouse for about 6 years and it was only while attempting to rob a pig drover from Llanddarog on Bristol Bridge that he was recognised and arrested. Years later his son was hanged for being involved in the robbery of his aunt and her attempted murder.'

31 March 1789 – William Griffith convicted of burglary – hung 18 April.

'The next hanging to take place was that of shoemaker Sioni'r Cornell, who in 1797 murdered his father at Llanfihangel, Abercowin. He swung at Pensarn. On 4th August, 1802 records show that a person had been placed in the pillory' (–*executionwales.blogspot*).

10 August 1798 – John William convicted of murder of his father, Lewis – hung 16 August.

Note: The blogspot *executionwales* also records the following, with reference to William Thomas, executed in 1773: 'On 28th March 1770, nine men were condemned to death at Hereford, before Mr Justice Yates and Baron Perrott, for the murder of William Powell of Glanareth, Llangadock, in his parlour on the 8th January. On the 22nd March, all nine men had been removed from Carmarthen Gaol and taken to Hereford by Habeas Corpus. Of the nine who had been tried, William Spiggott, (alias Spicket), William Morris, David Morris,

David Morgan, (alias Lacey), William Walter Evan, Charles David Morgan and David Llewellyn, of Llandovery, were found guilty and were all hanged in Hereford on 30th March. William Spiggott and William Walter Evan were later hanged in chains. William Thomas (alias Blink John Spiggott) and William Charles were both acquitted, but William Thomas returned to live in Carmarthen and was hanged at Pensarn for horse stealing. Walter Evan had turned King's evidence but it didn't stop him from being hanged later for further crimes.

Charles David Morgan was betrayed by footprints and blood in the snow which were traced to him, and typically he accused several of his accomplices. The evidence was given in Welsh, where it was claimed that William Williams was the instigator and ringleader of the gang. He was never brought before the court because he fled to France. William Powell had been murdered because William Williams wanted to marry Powell's wife. Of the twenty wounds inflicted on William Powell, it was proved by the prosecution that any one of eight would have caused death. At his funeral, his casket was covered in a scarlet cloth to show that he had been murdered.

Records also proved that William Powell's wife had planned her husband's murder, and the wife of William Williams was also aware that her husband was trying to kill her. On one occasion he had attempted to hang her while on another he put white powder into her tea. It was only that her child had said that Williams had put some sugar from his pocket into the cup that saved her. The tea was later given to the dog and days later it was dead. As to what became of Williams in France, he was taken prisoner by a French privateer, but again managed to escape and fled to St Omer were he became a school teacher. However he drowned when he took a party of school children on a cruise. In his parents' house at Boulogne, they discovered a pocket book with a blood spot and an entry on the page 8th

January, 1770 read "my finger bled today how singular." The story ends with the story of a man who had been interpreter at the court, who was fired at as he went home by a man disguised in an ass's skin who had jumped from the hedge. No record mentions a conviction for this crime.'

Chapter 6

A Note on Cardigan Offences

Cardigan – William Owen's home town – had a similar profile of sentences. The following pieces are from *A History of Cardigan, the Locality and its People*, (published by the *Cardigan & Tivy-Side Advertiser* from source material supplied by Donald Davies. Vol 2, 1992.)

'In 1775, Mary Eynon of St Mary's parish was convicted of petty larceny, her punishment was "to be stripped from the waist upwards and whipped in the porch of the common gaol, till your body 'be bloody' by the Master of the House of Correction." It seems the chairman of the local magistrates, Rev Dr Powell, preferred this to the alternative of putting her on the ducking stool and dipping her in the Teifi. In the following year, Susannah Daniel, wife of Daniel Daniel, was also similarly publicly whipped for petty larceny. In 1786, Thomas Davies, of Llangoedmor, was convicted of stealing clothing valued at 11d and also whipped as above, this time "until the blood flowed freely from his back". The punishment was repeated a week later, on a different route through the town. At the same Sessions as above, Margaret Davies, also of Llangoedmor, was sentenced to a single whipping for stealing a piece of brown cloth worth 6d.

In 1801, William Lewis of Llandysul was sentenced to death for stealing a ewe worth 5 shillings, this was later commuted to transportation for life and he ended up in NSW, Australia. Cardigan's only female transportee was Eleanor James, aged 24, she stole clothing from the house of an Ann Thomas in Tremain, the clothing belonging to the latter and one Mary Phillips. This wasn't Eleanor's first offence, she was transported in 1823 on the vessel *Brothers* with 89 others to Hobart, Tasmania. In 1827, William Andrews, a tramp, pleaded guilty to stealing "old garments" from a house in Aberporth, he was sentenced to death and was hanged at Cardigan County Gaol.

In 1826, Enoch Thomas and Owen Jones were to be found languishing in Cardigan County Gaol. Enoch had been found guilty of burglary, and sentenced to 2 years hard labour, and Owen of theft, and sentenced to 6 months hard labour. Their punishment included 8 hours daily on the dreaded treadmill. They were however excused hard labour on Christmas Day and Good Friday. In 1883, Eleanor Jones pleaded guilty to stealing notepaper and envelopes from a shop in Llandysul, was sentenced to 18 months hard labour, and the judge appeared to agree with her statement that she 'wouldn't come out alive'.

The last murder trial at Cardigan was held in 1885 when Sergeant Price of the Cardiganshire Militia was sentenced to death, for the murder of his wife during a quarrel. A person who stole clothing in Aberporth in 1827 was hung in the prison for his crime.'

Chapter 7

The Cwilt Conundrum

It was believed by the poor across Wales that if someone could build a house on common land in one night (*un nos*), the property and would be theirs as a freehold. One tradition was that if a fire burning was burning in the hearth by the following morning, the new 'owner' could extend his land around the house by the distance he could throw an axe from the four corners of the property. From the 17th-19th centuries, land enclosures, taxation by landowners, poverty and an expanding population brought about such squatting in isolated rural parts of Wales. Most *tai unnos* were quickly made of turf and soil, with a roughly thatched roof. If left alone, the occupants usually replaced the walls with clay and stone. The *tŷ unnos* (one night house) had no legal status but was often tolerated, and some remain across the country, such as the famed Tŷ Hyll (Ugly House) near Capel Curig in Snowdonia.

In the early eighteenth century, Siôn Cwilt was a folk hero in Ceredigion, building such a *tŷ unnos* near Synod Inn, where there is an area still known as Banc Siôn Cwilt. The River Clettwr rises in two streams from the moorland, and some say that the *banc* had its name from a hermit who made his abode there, dressed in patch-work rags, hence known as 'Johnny Quilt'. The legend of a hermit may be confused with that of the smuggler Siôn Cwilt. It was also thought that this Siôn built his tiny cottage here because it was between Ffynnonbedr (Peterwell Mansion), owned by his relative Sir Herbert Lloyd, and two Ceredigion beaches he used for smuggling – Cwmtydu and Cei Bach. (Synod Inn is not 5 miles from Cwmtydu beach and around 14 miles from Lloyd's Lampeter manor). However, this popular law-breaker was supposed to operate from a derelict cottage near Cwmtydu, and known as Twm Siôn Cwilt, with reference to Twm Siôn Cati, the 'Welsh Robin Hood' who died in 1609.

W.J. Lewis of Aberystwyth recounted the following to Bethan Phillips: 'According to tradition Peterwell mansion was well supplied with many luxuries such as casks of brandy, French wines, tea, tobacco, sugar, silks and many other fineries supplied by the smugglers. One of the most notable of the Cardiganshire smugglers was Siôn Cwilt, whose name is still associated with the tract of moorland between New Quay and Llandysul. He built himself a *Tŷ Unos* inland from Cwmtydu, living the life of a recluse. At first he dressed as a gentleman, but in time his clothes became worn and patched until his cloak resembled a quilt. Hence the name Siôn Cwilt. People came to fear him and believed him to have associations with the devil. Among the few visitors who came at dead of night to his cabin, was the infamous Sir Herbert Lloyd of Peterwell. It was also noticed that servants from Peterwell would visit Siôn and return to Lampeter with a waggon fully laden with sacks, bottles and casks. Sir Herbert was not the only member of the gentry to approach the cabin, for it was the centre of a brisk smuggling trade, enabling the finest brandies and wines to appear on the tables of the Cardiganshire squires.'

Sir Herbert Lloyd (1719–1769), MP for Cardiganshire Borough, and first Baronet of Peterwell, Cardiganshire, was a notorious figure, making his own justice, and like many landowners and dignitaries profited from smuggling. [He was never Sheriff of Cardiganshire, as many write]. As a JP, Lloyd ordered Ann Morgan to be stripped to the waist and tied to the back of a cart, for being found 'idle and disorderly' in Lampeter. She was whipped along the 'whipping route' between the Green Dragon inn and Thomas Daniel's house in early October 1750. Lloyd ordered that she be stripped 'from the waiste upwards and whipped in the open market between the hours of ten in the morning and three in the afternoon in the Town of Lampeter and back again until her body be bloody.' He next ordered that the same Ann Morgan be 'likewise whipped on 15 October in the town of Aberystwyth from the Market House to the bridge and back again and that in the meantime she be kept in the custody of the Gaoler'. In 1755 Lloyd was struck from the Commission of the Peace, for illegal abuse of his authority. Like William Owen, he was an enemy of Thomas Johnes of Abermâd, sending word as 'his bosom friend' to meet him in Llanybydder on a matter of business. With 100 men, he assaulted the unsuspecting Johnes, and took him to Cardigan Gaol.

A contemporary account reads that Johnes was 'dragged to Bronwydd. The following morning he was taken to Cardigan where he was kept on display opposite the hall, bound on the back of a horse for everyone to stare at him. He was then placed in a beer house for two or three days... with armed men as sentries, and when his son came looking for him, he was really hammered... he was then carried to gaol.' Johnes ended up in London's Fleet Prison for three years, being released in 1760. In 1762 he was stealing cattle from neighbouring farmers. As master of Peterwell, Lampeter, Lloyd was a hated tyrant. His treatment of his second wife forced her to leave him, he was said to have had a farmer executed on false charges as he wanted his land, and gambling losses forced him to mortgage most of his great estate. 'At the general election of 1768 a coalition against Lloyd was formed among the Cardiganshire gentry, and though he canvassed both county and borough in 1769 he was unseated as an MP.'

In great debt, inside his four-turreted country seat with a unique roof garden, he was defiant to his creditors. As Phillips writes, 'any person bearing a writ to the mansion was forced to cram it into his mouth, and was then unceremoniously horse-whipped down the Portland marble stapes, glad to flee for his life.' He is also noted for having a Lampeter farmer, Siôn ap Philip, hanged because he wanted his land, and the field he took is still called Cae Siôn Philip. Lloyd died in 1769, and his great mansion fell into ruins. From time to time bottles are unearthed at the site, once filled by Siôn Cwilt's wine, and with Sir Herbert Lloyd's name embossed on the seals.

It appears that Siôn Cwilt's real name was John White, and that his nickname of 'Cwilt' came from his colourful coats or cloaks. He was said to have worn a quilted coat to keep out the chill of the night while he was unloading goods on the shore. However, it may be a corruption of *gwyllt* (wild). The name John Qwilt appears in Llanina parish minutes, recording the baptism of his son there in 1758. Another of his nicknames was Siôn *Sais* (Englishman, deriving from Saxon), indicating that he was not able to speak Welsh fluently. Like much of the west Wales coastline, Cwmtydu and Cei Bach were remote and suitable for secretive operations at night. Cwilt, armed with a sword and a gun, would ride his horse to meet the smugglers' boats. Important local people like Sir Herbert Lloyd depended on smuggling for their wines and spirits, and to a great extent would defend their suppliers from the customs officers.

Armed men patrolled the coast to prevent smuggling, and nearby New Quay had 'watch houses', where toll men kept watch for smugglers' boats. Apart from smuggling, Cwilt was said to sack ships from Ireland and France, laden with salt, tobacco, perfumes, brandy and wines, which ran aground on the coast. Goods were heavily taxed and salt was a particularly expensive commodity needed for the herring trade. Coastguards, known as horse riders, were often English, non-Welsh speakers, disliked by local communities, who helped Cwilt when he was confronted by them.

There was another smuggler associated with Sir Herbert Lloyd and Cwmtydu, recounted to Bethan Phillips by D.G. Williams of Llannon: 'This is a traditional story told in the New Quay area and it links Sir Herbert Lloyd with the activities of the smugglers who infested the Cardiganshire coastline during this period. Shâms Pant yr Ynn was a local rascal, grossly immoral, who had fathered so many bastards that he was a liability to the area and a burden on the parish. He was also Sir Herbert's contact with the smugglers; but Sir Herbert had long been dissatisfied with him on account of his boastful nature and his many indiscretions. One evening, Sir Herbert rode down to Cwmtydu and caught Shâms in the act of selling his wife to the smugglers. The Baronet saw his opportunity of ridding himself of Shâms. He ordered a makeshift gallows to be erected on the beach, and had him hanged there as an example to others.'

T. Llew Jones, in his novel *Dirgelwch yr Ogof* (1977) recounts the legend of Sion Cwilt as a local squire's son, who turned smuggler after irredeemable losses at sea threaten the family's tenure at Glascoed. Gillian Morgan, in a blog on *americymru.net*, relates that the man known as Siôn Cwilt came to a cottage overlooking the sea bringing with him twenty or more ponies. 'Visiting one of the inns close to the beach, he confided that he was expecting a boat from Roscoff [Brittany] to arrive within a few days. He needed men to help him unload the cargo quickly, under cover of darkness, in order to avoid the government's 'Excise Men', who patrolled the area. One afternoon in September, 1797, a lugger from Roscoff dropped anchor in the bay. When night fell, the boat drew closer to the shore, where Siôn Cwilt and his men were waiting with the ponies. By daybreak, the French boat had sailed away and the kegs of brandy were hidden in caves. Soon, stories began to circulate that smuggling was taking place, but no-one in Cwmtydu, when questioned, was prepared to speak to the Excise Men. Siôn Cwilt's activities continued, until a man named Daniel Ifan tried to sell brandy in Llangrannog. Daniel Ifan's capture and subsequent hanging brought an end to Siôn Cwilt's reign in Cwmtydu and he left the area.'

The *Ceredigion.gov* website repeats the same story for 1797: 'When the new day began the French boat had sailed away, the kegs of brandy and other goods hidden in the caves. The smuggler who organised the venture was Siôn Cwilt known for the many dark nights he waited at the cottage for the boats to arrive loading the alcohol, tobacco, tea and salt onto his ponies. The people of Cwmtydu would whisper amongst themselves about Siôn Cwilt the smuggler in the colourful quilted coat, but no one would tell the Sheriff of the County. Sometime later a man named Daniel Ifans was caught and arrested in Llangrannog for selling smuggled brandy. He was found guilty and hung. Siôn Cwilt disappeared from the secluded cove at Cwmtydu, his reign of smuggling over. He was never seen here again.' Unfortunately there is no record of Daniel Ifans (or Evans) being executed anywhere in Wales in the 18th century, and 1797 is too late for Cwilt to be associated with Sir Herbert Lloyd. The tale is confusing – was there a hermit by the same name at Synod Inn, or could it be that Cwilt (if he existed) spent his 'retirement' here? However, in 2016 the headmistress of the local primary school at Synod Inn, named Ysgol Gymunedol Bro Siôn Cwilt, has kept up the Cwilt tradition. She was struck off the teaching register 'for plundering school funds, to pay for personal spending'.

Chapter 8

The Rebecca Rioter who owned Cae Lilly

In *Rebecca and her Daughters*, by H.T. Evans, 1910, we read that in June 1843: '... a letter signed by "Eliza," and dated at Conwil, was delivered by an unknown man to a certain person at Llandyssul. The writer commanded him to summon all the inhabitants of the village to meet the writer that night at the gate of Llanfihangel-Yeroth. The recipient of the letter, thoroughly alarmed at the consequences threatened should he disobey, hastily sent the Crier to publish the contents of the letter throughout the village. Eliza kept her appointment and passed through Llandyssul with a large party, who were disguised and armed with guns which they discharged at intervals. A great number of the peaceably-disposed inhabitants of Llandyssul, struck with terror at Eliza's threat, joined Rebecca's children and marched to the Llanfihangel-Yeroth Gate, a distance of three miles, where all were "compelled to labour hard in the work of destruction, amid the cheers, howlings, and sometimes horrid screeches of Rebecca and her children." In a short time the gate-posts, etc., were entirely destroyed and carried away by the crowd...

On 16th July Rebecca and her family mustered about 200 strong in the neighbourhood of Llanybyther and New Inn, and destroyed the Gwarallt Gate, not far from the latter place on the Carmarthen and Lampeter Road, and also another bar. Rebecca on this occasion was gaily dressed, and sported a parasol. When the work of demolition was complete, the party quickly dispersed over the hills. A bridge near Cross Inn was also destroyed, and the scaffolding of a bridge about to be erected at Cwmgwili; but it appears that Rebecca did not confine her enmity to turnpike-gates and bridges, as about this time she demolished three gates leading to a Dissenting chapel in the upper part of Carmarthenshire...

13th July. The Summer Assizes opened before Sir Robert Monsy Rolfe. On Tuesday, the 16th, David Evans was tried for being concerned in pulling down and destroying Llanfihangel-ar-arth Gate, and found "Guilty of being in the company, but not guilty of demolishing." On Wednesday (17th) he was again tried for destroying Gwarallt Gate [and toll house]. The jury having been locked up all night, and not agreeing, the judge ordered the prisoner to be discharged, but told him that he might be called again at the next, or any other Assizes to be tried for the same offence before another jury.'

The Welshman, and General Advertiser for the Principality of Wales 18 July 1844 reported: 'The Grand Jury here brought in two true bills against David Evans, for demolishing a turnpike gate and toll house; they were then discharged by His Lordship. There were nine causes on the cause list, but as none of them were quite ready for trial in consequence of the non-arrival of the witnesses, the court was adjourned at a quarter past three o'clock, till nine the following morning.

TUESDAY. David Evans, farmer, was charged with having, on the 19th of June, 1843, feloniously and riotously demolished the dwelling-house of David Thomas, situate at Llanfihangel. There were several counts in the indictment which stated the house to be the house of David Thomas, and the house of the Carmarthen and Tivyside District of Roads. The prosecution was conducted by Messrs. Chilton, Q.C., and E. V. Williams. The prisoner was defended by Mr. E. C. Lloyd Hall. Mr. Chilton in addressing the jury for the prosecution, said, that the prisoner was a farmer occupying a farm at a rent of 1:60 a year, and was charged with having assisted on the 19th of June, 1813, in demolishing the dwelling-house of David Thomas, or in other words, the toll-house of the Llanfihangel gate. David Thomas who was the toll collector, slept in the house on the night of Sunday, the 18th of June, but in consequence of it having been proclaimed at the breaking of a gate in the neighbourhood that the Llanfihangel gate was to be pulled down on the Monday night, he removed his furniture on the Monday morning.

On the Monday night a large mob came, disguised and armed, and attacked the house. The first person who attacked it was the prisoner, who broke the upper window with the muzzle of his gun. They then broke the gate, and pulled down the house, leaving scarcely any of the walls standing. The prisoner took a leading part, and gave orders in English, and was seen marching up and down and occasionally firing his gun. The evidence against him would be that of three persons who were present and who might be called by the prisoner's counsel accomplices. He should prove what the prisoner said when he was committed for trial; and where he was concealed when he was apprehended, and what he said to the magistrate who committed him. It might be asked (continued Mr. C.) what was the reason this case was not brought on before? To this he would answer that the system of intimidation was such that it was a very long time before anyone connected with the Rebecca riots was brought to justice. In conclusion he would say that there had been a widely spread rumour that the juries of Carmarthenshire would not do their duty. He was happy to say that they had afforded the most complete refutation of those rumours by their conduct at the late Assizes. He called on the jury therefore to do their duty now fearlessly, but should they have a fair and reasonable doubt, he implored them to give it in favour of the prisoner.

The following witnesses were then examined in support of

the case for the prosecution. Thomas Jones, Dolmain, – I am a farm servant. I remember Monday night, 19th June, 1843 – the night Llanfihangel gate was broken. I heard that the gate was to be broken, and I went to see it. It was about 10 o'clock at night when I went. I saw a number of persons coming between 12 and 1 o'clock. I had waited till then. They were disguised some had women's clothes on, and were like ladies. Some had their hats tied to look like bonnets. Their faces were coloured greyish black. I knew David Evans, the prisoner. He was dressed in white. His face was coloured. I knew him, and was near enough to him. I saw him break the upper window of the Llanfihangel toll-house. He broke it with the muzzle of a double barrelled gun. The crowd were round about him. Prisoner was talking in English I did not understand. The mob, after he had addressed them in English, broke the gate. They pulled the toll house down afterwards. I stayed there nearly all the time till the mob had gone. Prisoner was firing his gun while they were pulling the house down. They were all crying out. There were a great many people there more than fifty disguised. I was not disguised. I was in my customary clothes. I had known prisoner before. I was standing by the wall close to the window when he put the gun through it. I knew his walk. He walked up and down, while they were breaking the house. I knew his voice.

Cross-examined by Mr. Hall: It was a fine night. Tolerably light. There were a good many waiting there for them. I did not see David Jones, Blaenman, nor Evan Evans, Bribwll. I did not remain in the same place. I walked backwards and forwards. My master's name is John Lloyd. I have been in his service from All Hollandtide till now. I do not know of a quarrel between the prisoner and my master. I heard that Wernmacwydd gate had been broken. I did not hear that prisoner had been taken as a witness to prove who broke it. I do not know that John Lloyd was charged with breaking it. Once I saw the window broken.

It was the prisoner did it. I am positive, I did not see John Jones, of Cross Inn, there. I do not know that he was employed to watch the gate.

David Jones: I remember 19th June, 1843. I went to bed as it was getting dark on that night. After I was in bed my wife awoke me, and I heard shots fired, and holloaing out. They were knocking at the window and the door. I went down and opened the upper half of the door. It was a fine night. I saw 3 or 4 people in the doorway. They were dressed in strange clothes, similar to women's clothes. They had men's voices, their faces were coloured. They asked me for pick-axes, in English. They said mattocks. I said I did not understand them. Another man asked then in Welsh for a pickaxe. One had a gun; which was held opposite my person across the half door while they asked me for the mattock. They told me to dress, and that I should have not much time to dress. I was frightened. They said I must go with them. I did go with them to Llanfihangel gate. The first thing I heard was the window broken. I was too far behind to see who did it. There was a small gate further on, and they broke that first. I did not see them, but heard them at it. I saw the Llanfihangel gate being pulled down, when they came back from the small gate.

I heard a person talking in English. I did not know him, nor understand him. I saw prisoner amongst them. I have known him 15 years. He had a woman's gown on. His face was coloured. He asked me to throw aside some sticks that had been taken down from the roof of the house. I knew his voice. He had a gun. I saw them pulling down the house. There were a great number many of them disguised. I heard prisoner telling them to work. He told them in English. He fired shots now and then. Others fired shots now and then. There was a great deal of noise and disturbance. The house was about half destroyed. All the roof and beams were taken away. Cross-examined by

Mr. Hall: My face was not blackened. No one asked me to black my face or holloa. I remained till they had finished. About an hour. John Lloyd, of Dolmain, is a landlord of mine. I know Evan Rees, Bribwll. He is no relation of mine, but he is a neighbour. I know John Oliver. I do not know that they were charged with breaking Wernmacwydd gate. I heard something about it. But I do not know anything about it. I cannot say whether prisoner was to be a witness against them.

Evan Evans: I remember the night the gate was broken. I was undressing to go to bed that night when a person in disguise came to the door of my house and ordered me to go with him to Llanfihangel-gate. I was not willing, I was tired. He said I was bound to go. My wife said I had better go for fear she and the children might be endangered. I went with him, and on the turnpike road scores were assembled.

Some had guns and some had disguises. They fired the guns and made a great noise. We went to Cross Inn. Before we got there I recognised the prisoner. He had something white over his shoulders, and his face coloured dark. He had a gun in his hand. I was talking to him. I knew him before. I was a tenant of his. I had put something over one side of my face myself. I said "David is it you are here?" and he told me not to call any person by his name. We then went to the Llanfihangel gate. Prisoner was there. Some days after I saw the prisoner he was not disguised then. I spoke to him about knocking the gate down. I said "There was a terrible appearance at the toll-house." He said they had worked well there. He gave me a letter some days after, and asked me to take it and to leave it at the smith's shop at Cross-Inn fach. Cross-examined by Mr. Hall: I did not see all that took place. I saw the first window broken. It was the upper window. That was done before the gate was demolished. I do not know who broke it. I do not think it was prisoner. It was a short man. The window I saw broken was broken by a man shorter than prisoner. I heard of no dispute between John Lloyd and prisoner. I heard someone say, we will meet Becca at Cross Inn. That was half a mile from Cross Inn, further from Llanfihangel. I asked prisoner to go to the farm yard at Cross Inn to see Becca pass. He did not come with me. I went on to Cross Inn and saw the people pass. I can't say where prisoner was then. I had lost sight of him. Re-examined: I cannot say whether the window was broken with a stick or a gun. The prisoner was disguised.

David Thomas: I remember the night when the Llanfihangel gate was destroyed. I had been toll collector before then. I lived in the house, and slept in the house the night before the gate was destroyed. I had occupied the house 24 years. I rented the tolls. I heard a report that the house was to be pulled down, and I moved my furniture on Monday morning. On the night of that day the house was pulled down. I paid rent to the Carmarthen and Tivyside District of Roads. John Timothy Hughes, Superintendent of Rural Police: On the 27th May I conveyed prisoner to gaol. I did not hold out any hope or threat. He said it was hard that he should suffer when he did no more than the others. He said it in Welsh. He had been committed for trial, and he was speaking about the gate business. Cross-examined: He complained several times. I had no conversation about other gates. I had no conversation with him. I only listened to what he said. He spoke about the Llanfihangel and Gwarallt gates. I understood him to speak of both, as he was committed for both.

Henry Roberts, Police Officer: I had a warrant to apprehend prisoner at the bar, on the 24th of May. I searched for him, and found him in David Jones's house, concealed in a corner of a bedroom upstairs. That was on the 12th of May. It was about nine in the morning. He was in bed, and had his clothes on. Cross-examined: I am stationed at Pencader. I heard on that morning that he had been to Carmarthen the day before. I heard he had been about Mr. Bowen, of Wernmacwydd.

John Lloyd Davies, Esq., magistrate for the county of Carmarthen: I took the examination of the witnesses, some portion myself. I took down the examination of David Jones. I asked prisoner whether he wished to put questions to David Jones. I did not take down the answer. I asked him if he had any question to ask the witness. I have only to say I was there, but did no more than others. He said it in Welsh. Cross-examined by Mr. Hall: I translated the proceedings into English myself. A stranger came in, and said he came with David Evans. I asked if he was a professional man. He said no. I then requested the room to be cleared. Re-examined: He can speak a little English. He is a farmer.

Mr. Hall addressed the jury for the prisoner. He said there was no doubt that the toll house and gate were destroyed; and that a vast number of persons assembled and made a great noise and riot, but there was a great doubt that the prisoner had helped to pull the house down, or that he was a party to the riot. He commented on the fact that the third witness had positively denied the prisoner to be the man who broke the window. Was that not a sufficient matter of doubt for the jury? The prisoner had perhaps been drawn there by the mob out of curiosity, and did not assist to demolish the house. The conversations amounted to nothing at all. The delay in bringing the prisoner to justice proved more than the mere love of truth and justice, and would the jury lend themselves to countenance a matter that the Government had not thought fit to bring forward. The learned Counsel concluded by calling on the jury to acquit the prisoner, and send him home rejoicing to his family a happier and a wiser man.

The learned Judge in summing up observed, that there could be no doubt the house had been demolished according to the meaning of the statute. It was equally clear that it was so demolished on the night of the 19th or rather early on the 20th of July. There was also no doubt, that there was a large mob tumultuously and riotously assembled, and if the evidence of the different witnesses was true, there could be no doubt that the prisoner was there also. In fact he might say there was no doubt about the prisoner being there. But his being there was not sufficient to show that he was a guilty participator in all that was done there. The mere fact of his being there was capable of explanation, but the question was whether he was there and taking part in what was going on, either by giving directions, or urging the others on, or even of intimidating peaceable people from preventing them. His Lordship then read the evidence, and observed that there was nothing in the demeanour of the witnesses to lead to the supposition that they were telling a false story. In conclusion he would tell them that if they thought the prisoner was there aiding and encouraging the mob to demolish the house, they must find him guilty but if they were not satisfied of that they must find him not guilty. The jury retired for about three hours, and then returned a verdict of Not Guilty.

WEDNESDAY. David Evans, of Penlan, farmer, who was on Tuesday acquitted for the felony of destroying Llanfihangel toll house and gate, was again placed at the bar and charged with the misdemeanour of destroying the Gwarallt-gate, in the parish of Llanllwny. Messrs. Chilton, Q. C., and E. V. Williams appeared for the prosecution, and E. C. Lloyd Hall defended the prisoner. Mr. Chilton stated the case for the prosecution, and said that the prisoner was charged under the statute of 7 and 8 Geo. IV. for having destroyed a turnpike gate, and he was also charged with a riot. On the night of the 10th of July, 1843, the Gwarallt gate was destroyed. In the afternoon of that day the prisoner called on a man named John Oliver, and desired him with threats to attend and assist in the demolition of the gate. About 10 o'clock in the evening of the same day, the prisoner called in disguise on Evan Rees, whom he found in bed, and told him if he did not get up and come to assist in destroying the gate, his house should be on fire before the following morning. He also called on Thomas Davies, of Cross-Inn-fach, and threatened him likewise. The three accompanied the prisoner to the gate and when there they saw an immense number of people armed and disguised, having their faces blackened. The prisoner had a double barrelled gun, and he set the people to work to break the gate. There were two parties in the crowd, one disguised and engaged in breaking the gate, and the other looking on.

The prisoner kept these latter at bay, and said he had sixty loads of cartridge: He even shot at a boy, who was, however, not wounded. The iron gate was completely destroyed before the mob left. After the several witnesses had been examined, Mr. Hall addressed the jury for the prisoner, and commented with great severity on the discrepancies between the evidence of the witnesses and their depositions before the magistrates. He denominated it a gross and vile conspiracy, and said that perjury had been committed by the witnesses for the prosecution. The reason why this charge had been so long delayed was, that the parties who were the witnesses in this case had been accused by the prisoner of participating in the destruction of the Wernmacwydd gate, and this charge was then trumped up by them in order to get the prisoner out of the way, so that he should not be a witness against them. The first witness contradicted himself in three places, and the second witness did so in two places. These were important discrepancies. He would prove that Rees, (the first witness) on the Saturday before the gate was broken, was met by one James James, to whom he said he intended to break the gate, and would take his cross saw with him. He should also prove that on the night in question Oliver, (the second witness) called on the prisoner, although Oliver had sworn that he had only seen the prisoner at two places, neither of them being his own house. The learned Counsel concluded by making a powerful appeal to the Jury to acquit the prisoner.

Mr. Chilton replied at some length, and his Lordship then proceeded to sum up. The Jury retired at 11 o'clock in the forenoon. At about eight in the evening, after the court was adjourned, His Lordship was recalled, and the jury delivered a verdict that the prisoner was Not guilty of breaking the gate. His Lordship explained that the prisoner was not charged with breaking the gate, but was charged with riotously assembling with others, with intent to demolish the gate. The jury were then sent back to reconsider their verdict. At two o'clock in the morning, His Lordship was aroused from his bed by the jury, who stated that they had agreed on their verdict. When, however, His Lordship arrived at the Town Hall, it was found that the jury had not agreed. At nine o'clock on Thursday morning, His Lordship, finding there was no probability of the jury agreeing to a verdict, dismissed them, and told the prisoner he would be tried by a fresh jury on a future occasion. The prisoner was discharged, after having notice given him that he would be told when a charge would be preferred against him.'

The Cambrian reported upon the Carmarthen Summer Assizes of 20 July 1844: 'The business of the Court commenced this morning at nine o'clock. David Evans, farmer, the person acquitted on the preceding day on the charge of demolishing a turnpike-gate and toll-house, day on the charge of demolishing a turnpike-gate and toll-house, which amounted to a transportable felony, was this morning tried on a charge of misdemeanour. The indictment charged him with having, on Sixteenth July, 1843, riotously and tumultuously assembled, with divers other persons, and demolished Gwarallt turnpike gate. Mr. Chilton, Q.C., addressed the jury for the prosecution. From the Learned Gentleman's statement, which was subsequently confirmed by the evidence of the witnesses for the prosecution, it appeared that a short time previous to the destruction of the gate, the prisoner called upon a person named Oliver, and commanded him, at the peril of having his house fired, to come and assist in the destruction of the gale. He also called on a Person named Evan Rees, of Bribwll, and held out similar threats to him. He also used threats towards one Thomas Davies, of Cross Inn farm, and insisted upon his disguising himself, which the latter positively declined doing.

One of the witnesses accompanied the prisoner to the gate, where he saw a large assemblage of persons, the majority of whom were disguised. The prisoner was also disguised, his face having been blackened, and his body covered with a grey dress. He was armed with a double-barrelled gun. The crowd appeared to be divided into two divisions, one of which was engaged in breaking the gate, and the other composed principally of spectators and lookers-on. The prisoner was engaged in forming the spectators into a ring, and in keeping them off, so as to prevent their pressing upon the other division, consisting of disguised persons, who were actively engaged in demolishing the gate. One of the witnesses deposed to the prisoner having said to the mob, "Be of good cheer, I have sixty more rounds." Mr. Chilton concluded by referring to some observations which had been made on the preceding trial, about the serious consequences to the prisoner of a conviction. In this case, he was happy to inform the jury, the prisoner was charged with a misdemeanour only, not that he thought the jury had anything to do with consequences, for it was the duty of juries to act according to the evidence, whatever the consequences might be.

Mr. Lloyd Hall defended the prisoner, and directed his cross-examination principally to the support of alleged discrepancies between the evidence of the witnesses in Court, and their depositions before the Magistrates. Witnesses were also called to depose to statements made to them by the witnesses for the prosecution contradictory of their evidence in Court. Mr Hall in his address to the jury designated the prosecution a conspiracy against the prisoner, because it was well-known that the prisoner had laid an information against some of the witnesses who were alleged (but they denied it) to have been engaged in the destruction of Wernmacwydd gate. The jury retired at twelve o clock, and were locked up until half-past eight in the evening, when a message was sent that they had agreed. The Sheriff's carriage was immediately dispatched for his Lordship, who had gone to dine at Glannant (the seat of J. Wilson, Esq.) After his Lordship's arrival, the jury appeared in Court, and returned a verdict "Not Guilty" of breaking the gate. His Lordship asked "Gentleman, the charge is that of having riotously assembled for the purpose of breaking the gate. He is not charged with having himself broken it." A Juryman answered "There are nine against three – we are all agreed but those three. His Lordship – "Gentlemen, you must be locked up again. The jury were then locked up.

THURSDAY. At two o'clock this morning, the jury in the case of David Evans, having been locked up during the whole night, sent a messenger for the Learned Judge to his lodgings. His Lordship got out of his bed, and soon arrived at The Townhall. On learning that there was no probability of their coming to a verdict, the Learned Judge read the whole of the evidence over again – in fact, made a second summing up, – at the conclusion of which, the jury again retired. On opening the business at nine o'clock, the jury again appeared in Court, and announced the fact of their not being able to agree upon a verdict. His Lordship told them that it did not appear to him they tried to agree, he should therefore dismiss them. The prisoner should also be discharged, but would be liable to be again brought to trial, of which (should that course be taken) he should receive due notice.'

References

Atholl Papers (MS09707) comprise a large archive of documents primarily relating to the administration of the Island during this period. The Lordship of Man descended to the Dukes of Atholl in 1736 and it was held by them until the Revestment in 1765.

Breverton, Terry, *The Book of Welsh Pirates and Buccaneers*, Glyndŵr Publishing 2003

Breverton, Terry, *The Pirate Handbook*, Glyndŵr Publishing 2004

Breverton, Terry, *Welsh Pirates and Privateers*, Gwasg Careg Gwalch, 2018

Elias, Twm, and Meirion, Dafydd, *Smugglers in Wales*, Gwasg Carreg Gwalch 2007, 2017

Evans, Titus and Elizabeth papers, Vols 1-5, *MS35, MS39, MS40* (transcripts of the Nevern Parish Register for baptisms, marriages and burials), Llyfrgell Genedlaethol Cymru – The National Library of Wales

Isle of Man Ingates and Outgates Records: This series of documents records the receipts from custom duties on both imports to and exports from the island. A booklet of Ingates and Outgates was produced each year by the water-bailiff, and the income generated was incorporated into the Rushen (South Side) Charge Book. The net receipts paid for salaries and grew to several thousands of pounds by the eighteenth century.

Jarvis, R.C., Customs Letter Book of the Port of Liverpool, 1711-1813, Chetham Society, 1954

Jones, Francis, *Bowen of Pentre Ifan and Llwyngwair*, The Pembrokeshire Historian, Journal of the Pembrokeshire Local History Society Vol 6, 1979 courtesy NLW online – Llyfrgell Genedlaethol Cymru – The National Library of Wales

Jones, Francis, *Llanreithan*, Pembrokeshire Historian Vol. 3, 1970

Muskett, Paul, *English Smuggling in the Eighteenth Century*, unpublished OU PhD thesis, 1996

Muskett, Paul, *Criminal Lives as Historical Evidence: The Case of William Owen, Smuggler, Slaver, Privateer and Murderer*, Isle of Man Studies Vol XIII, 2014-2015

Parry, Glyn, *Autobiography of a smuggler*, National Library of Wales Journal, 24, pp. 84-92 – Llyfrgell Genedlaethol Cymru – The National Library of Wales

Phillips, Bethan, *Peterwell – the History of a Mansion and its Infamous Squire*, Gomer, 1983

Platt, Richard, *Smuggling in the British Isles: A History* 2011 (plus Platt's superb website smuggling.co.uk)

Rodger, N.A.M., *The Wooden World: An Anatomy of the Georgian Navy*, London 1986

Vincent, Reverend Henry, *The History of St Dogmael's*, unpublished ms. 1860, Llyfrgell Genedlaethol Cymru – The National Library of Wales

Wilkins, Frances, *The Isle of Man in Smuggling History*, Wyre Forest Press, 1992

Websites – there are many wonderful resources, too many to mention, but the following are excellent sites:

capitalpunishment.org/Carmarthen

cindyvallar.com/smuggling is part of a brilliant pirate site

crime and punishment website, National Library of Wales

rhiw.com is dedicated to activated on the Llŷn, and has an excellent section on smugglers and smuggling, with excellent, well-researched contributions from O.J. Cowell

smuggling.co.uk, mentioned above under Platt, Richard